MYSTERIES OF GENESIS

BY CHARLES FILLMORE

Martino Publishing
Mansfield Centre, CT
2014

Martino Publishing
P.O. Box 373,
Mansfield Centre, CT 06250 USA

ISBN   978-1-61427-645-6

© *2014 Martino Publishing*

Cover design by T. Matarazzo

Printed in the United States of America On 100% Acid-Free Paper

MYSTERIES
OF GENESIS

BY CHARLES FILLMORE

UNITY SCHOOL OF CHRISTIANITY
KANSAS CITY, MISSOURI
1936

FOREWORD

Attention has been called to the need of a metaphysical textbook on Genesis, the world's best known and perhaps least understood allegory. A work of such a nature, if the entire book of Genesis were to be analyzed in detail, would be a great undertaking and fill a large volume. Therefore it was decided to prepare a book that would deal with the "high lights" or more important points of Genesis, omitting genealogies and such matters as would interest those trying to establish a historical interpretation. This would keep the work uniform with our other books in size and cost, at the same time furnishing a primary textbook to meet the needs of our students and friends.

The first three chapters of Genesis are covered in some detail because nothing is more important to the Truth student than an understanding of the creative process as it operates both in the original creation of man and in man's own creative activity. The remaining part of Genesis, as indeed the remainder of the Bible is the story of man's slow but certain rise from his fallen state in sense consciousness to his original perfection as the image of God. This development is traced through Noah, Abraham, Isaac, and

Jacob, down to Joseph, who is one of the best Old Testament examples of spiritual man in expression. The perfect expression of the restored and glorified I AM is the Christ, who became visible, lovable, and available to us in the personality of Jesus.

This metaphysical study is designed to show the origin of man as a perfect image or idea in Divine Mind; how this I AM image, called Jehovah God, forms the man idea into the man manifest, and how this man manifest must eventually become conscious both of his divine origin and his divine potentiality to become the God-man idea manifest, or the Christ.

Kansas City
1936

CONTENTS

Mysteries of Genesis

CHAPTER ONE

SPIRITUAL MAN

Study the 1st Chapter of Genesis.

Affirmative Prayer

The Spirit of wisdom and love, Elohim God, is within the secret depths of my being. I open my mind to His expression and seek to unify myself with His goodness, His love, and His wisdom.

Spiritual Man

THE BIBLE is the history of man. In its entire sixty-six books it describes in allegory, prophecy, epistle, parable, and poem, man's generation, degeneration, and regeneration. It has been preserved and prized beyond all other books because it teaches man how to develop the highest principle of his being, the spirit. As man is a threefold being, spirit, soul, and body, so the Bible is a trinity in unity. It is body as a book of history; soul as a teacher of morals; and spirit as a teacher of the mysteries of being.

The student of history finds the Bible interesting, if not wholly accurate; the faithful good man finds in it that which strengthens his righteousness, and the overcomer with Christ finds it to be the greatest of all books as a guide to his spiritual unfoldment. But it must be read in the Spirit in order to get its lesson. The key to its spiritual meaning is that back of every mentioned thing is an idea.

The Bible will be more readily understood if the fact be kept in mind that the words used have both an inner and an outer significance. Studied historically and intellectually, the external only is discerned, and the living inner reality is overlooked. In these lessons we shall seek to understand and to reveal the within, and trace the lawful and orderly connection between the within and the without.

Genesis, historically considered, has three parts: first, from the creation to the Flood; second, from the Flood to the call of Abraham; and third, from the call of Abraham to the death of Joseph.

The 1st chapter describes creation as accomplished in six days, and refers to a seventh day of rest. There is no reason to believe that these days were twenty-four hours in length. "One day is with the Lord as a thousand years, and a thousand years as one day." They simply represent periods of development or degrees of unfoldment.

Numbers are used throughout the Bible in connection with faculties or ideas in Divine Mind. There are twelve divine faculties. They are symbolized in the Old Testament by the twelve sons of Jacob and in the New Testament by the twelve disciples of Jesus Christ. All of these have a threefold character: first, as absolute ideas in Divine Mind; secondly, as thoughts, which are ideas in expression but not manifest; and thirdly, as manifestations of thoughts, which we call things. In man this threefold character is known as spirit, soul, and body. Therefore in studying man as the offspring of God it is necessary to distinguish between the faculties as they exist in the spirit and as they are expressed in the soul and manifested in the body. We find heaven to be the orderly arrangement of divine ideas within man's true being. Earth is the outer manifestation of those ideas, this manifestation being man's body.

The first step in the awakening of man to spiritual consciousness is the dawning of light, the perception of Truth through the quickening of his spirit. Light is wisdom, and the first day's work is the calling of light or wisdom into expression. Light represents intelligence, and darkness is undeveloped capacity. Symbolically these are "day" and "night."

The second step in mind is the development of faith or the "firmament." The "waters" represent the unestablished elements of the mind. The third step is the activity of the formative power of the mind called imagination. This gathers "the waters . . . together unto one place" so that the "dry land" appears. Then the imaginative faculty begins a great multiplication of forms and shapes in the mind.

The "two great lights" of the fourth day are the will and the understanding, or the sun (the spiritual I AM) and the moon (the intellect). These are but reflectors of the true light, for God had said, "Let there be light: and there was light"—before the sun and the moon were created.

The fifth step is the bringing forth of sensation and discrimination. The "creatures" are thoughts. The "birds . . . in the open firmament of heaven" are ideas approaching spiritual understanding.

The sixth step is the bringing forth of ideas after their kind. When man approaches creative power in his thought, he is getting close to God in his consciousness, and then the realization that he is the very image and likeness of his Creator dawns upon him. This is the consciousness in man of Christ.

The creation described in these six days, or six degrees or stages of God-Mind, is wholly spiritual and should not be confounded with the manifestation that is described in the succeeding chapters. God is mind, and all His works are created in mind as perfect ideas.

In the 1st chapter of Genesis it is the great creative Mind at work. The record portrays just how divine ideas were brought into expression. As man must first have an idea before he can bring an idea into manifestation, so it is with the creations of God. When a man builds a house he builds it first in his mind. He has the idea of a house, he completes the plan in his mind, and then he works it out in manifestation. Thus God created the universe. The 1st chapter of Genesis describes this ideal creation.

The 1st chapter shows two parts of the Trinity: mind, and idea in mind. In the 2d chapter we have the third part, manifestation. In this illustration all theological mystery about the Trinity is cleared away for we see that it is simply mind, idea in mind, and manifestation of idea. Since man is the offspring of God, made in the image and likeness of Divine Mind, he must express himself under the laws of this great creative mind. The law of manifestation for man is the law of thought. God ideates: man thinks. One is the completion of the other in mind.

The man that God created in His own image and likeness and pronounced good and very good is spiritual man. This man is the direct offspring of

Divine Mind, God's idea of a perfect man. This is
the only begotten Son, the Christ, the Lord God, the
Jehovah, the I AM. In the 2d chapter this Jehovah
or divine idea of perfect man forms the manifest
man and calls his name Adam.

The whole of the 1st chapter is a supermental
statement of the ideas upon which evolution is based.
Mind projects its ideas into universal substance, and
evolution is the manifestation of the ideas thus projected. The whole Genesiac record is an allegory
explaining just what takes place in the mind of each
individual in his unfoldment from the ideal to the
manifest. God, the great universal mind, brought
forth an idea, a man, perfect like Himself, and that
perfect man is potentially in every individual, working itself into manifestation in compliance with law.

INTERPRETATION OF THE BIBLE TEXT

1. In the beginning God created the heavens
and the earth.

The word "God" in this instance stands for
Elohim, which is God in His capacity as creative
power, including within Himself all the potentialities
of being. The "beginning" indicates the first concept of Divine Mind. "Created" means ideated.
The "heavens" is the realm of ideas, and the "earth"
represents ideas in expression. Heaven is the ideal
and earth the mental picture. A comparison is found
in the activity of our own mind: we have an idea and
then think out a plan before we bring it forth.

Ferrar Fenton, the well-known student of Hebrew and Greek, says that the first verse should read: "By periods God created that which produced the Suns; then that which produced the Earth. But the Earth was unorganized and empty; and darkness covered its convulsed surface; but the breath of God vibrated over its fluid face." From this we are to understand that God created, not the earth as it appears, but that which produced the earth. Elohim, Spirit, creates the spiritual idea, which is afterward made manifest through Jehovah God.

> 2. And the earth was waste and void; and the darkness was upon the face of the deep: and the Spirit of God moved upon the face of the waters.

The earthly thought was not yet clear. Harmony of form had not yet come into expression. "The deep" represents the capacity of the earth idea to bring forth. "The face of the deep" represents its intelligence. Understanding has not yet come into expression, and there is no apparent action. "The Spirit of God" or divine intelligence moved upon the "face of the waters." "Waters" here represents unexpressed capacities, the mental element out of which all is produced. Man is conscious of unexpressed capacities within himself, but only as he moves upon mind substance with intelligence, are his inherent spiritual qualities molded into forms.

> 3. And God said, Let there be light: and there was light.

"Light" is intelligence, a spiritual quality. It

corresponds to understanding and should precede all activity. In the beginning of any of our creating we should declare for light. Our declarations of Truth are instantly fulfilled in Spirit.

James says in his Epistle, "Every good gift and every perfect gift is from above, coming down from the Father of lights." John speaks of the "true light . . . which lighteth every man, coming into the world."

4. And God saw the light, that it was good: and God divided the light from the darkness.

All that emanates from God is good. In the process of bringing forth our ideas we need a certain degree of understanding in order properly to regulate our thoughts. The light must be divided from the darkness, as in Divine Mind the light was separated from the darkness.

5. And God called the light Day, and the darkness he called Night. And there was evening and there was morning, one day.

"Day" represents that state of mind in which intelligence dominates. "Night" represents the realm of thoughts that are not yet illuminated by the Spirit of God. "One day" represents a certain degree of mind unfoldment.

6. And God said, Let there be a firmament in the midst of the waters, and let it divide the waters from the waters.

The second day's creation is the second movement of Divine Mind. The central idea in this day's

creation is the establishment of a firmament in the
"midst of the waters" dividing the "waters from the
waters." "Waters" represent unexpected possibilities
in mind. There must be a "firm" starting point or
foundation established. This foundation or "firmament" is faith moving upon the unformed capacities
of Spirit consciousness. The divine Logos—God
as creative power—gives forth the edict "Let there
be a firmament." The first step or "day" in creation
involves "light" or understanding, and the second
step, faith in the knowing quality of mind.

> 7. And God made the firmament, and divided
> the waters which were under the firmament from
> the waters which were above the firmament: and it
> was so.

The word is instantly fulfilled in Spirit. "And
God made the firmament." This does not refer to
the visible realm of forms but to the mental image
in Divine Mind, which deals only with ideas. In
every mental state we have an "above" and a "below." Above the firmament are the unexpressed
capacities ("waters") of the conscious mind resting
in faith in Divine Mind. Below the firmament are
the unexpressed capacities ("waters") of the subconscious mind.

> 8. And God called the firmament Heaven.
> And there was evening and there was morning, a
> second day.

The word "Heaven" is capitalized in this passage
because it relates directly to Divine Mind. Faith

("firmament") established in consciousness is a state
of perfect harmony, therefore Heaven. Another
degree of mind unfoldment has been attained. "And
there was evening and there was morning, a second
day." "Evening" represents completion, and the
"morning" following represents activity of ideas.

> 9. And God said, let the waters under the
> heavens be gathered together unto one place, and
> let the dry land appear: and it was so.

The first day's creation reveals the light or inspiration of Spirit. The second day establishes faith
in our possibilities to bring forth the invisible. The
third day's creation or third movement of Divine
Mind pictures the activity of ideas in mind. This
is called expression. The formative power of mind
is the imagination, whose work is here represented
by the dry land. There is much unformed thought
in mind ("the heavens") that must be separated
from the formed.

> 10. And God called the dry land Earth; and
> the gathering together of the waters called he
> Seas: and God saw that it was good.

"Earth" is the mental image of formed thought
and does not refer to the manifest world. God is
Divine Mind and deals directly with ideas. "Seas"
represents the unformed state of mind. We say that
a man is "at sea" when he is in doubt in his mental
processes. In other words he has not established his
thoughts in line with the principle involved. The
sea is capable of production, but must come under

the dominion of the imagination.

11. And God said, Let the earth put forth grass, herbs yielding seed, *and* fruit-trees bearing fruit after their kind, wherein is the seed thereof, upon the earth: and it was so.

Divine Mind images its ideals definitely and in every detail. The ideal preceeds the fulfillment. "Let there be" represents the perfect confidence necessary to demonstration.

12. And the earth brought forth grass, herbs yielding seed after their kind, and trees bearing fruit, wherein is the seed thereof, after their kind: and God saw that it was good.

Ideas are productive and bring forth after their kind. They express themselves under the law of divine imagery. The seed is within the thought and is reproduced through thought activity until thought habits are formed. Thoughts become fixed in the earth or formed consciousness. In Divine Mind all is good.

13. And there was evening and there was morning, a third day.

Again a definite degree of mind unfoldment has been attained. Man, in forming his world, goes through the same mental process, working under divine law.

14. And God said, Let there be lights in the firmament of heaven to divide the day from the night; and let them be for signs, and for seasons, and for days and years.

The "firmament of heaven" is the consciousness
of Truth that has been formulated and established.
In the second day's creation a firmament was established in heaven (realm of divine ideas). This
firmament divides the day (illumined consciousness)
from the night (unillumined consciousness).
Through faith the "lights" are established; that is,
understanding begins to unfold. The "signs," "seasons," and "days and years" represent different stages
of unfoldment. We gain understanding by degrees.

15. And let them be for lights in the firmament
of heaven to give light upon the earth: and it
was so.

The "earth" represents the more external processes through which an idea passes, and corresponds
to the activity of an idea in mind. In man the
"earth" is the body consciousness, which in its real
nature is a harmonious expression of ideas established
in faith-substance. "And it was so"; that is, an idea
from divine consciousness is instantly fulfilled.

16. And God made the two great lights; the
greater light to rule the day, and the lesser light
to rule the night: *he made* the stars also.

The "greater light," in mind, is understanding
and the "lesser light" is the will. The greater light
rules "the day," that realm of consciousness which
has been illumined by Spirit. The lesser light rules
"the night," that is, the will; which has no illumination ("light" or "day") but whose office is to
execute the demands of understanding. The will

does not reason, but in its harmonious relation acts easily and naturally upon the inspiration of Spirit. Divine will expresses itself as the I AM in man.

The "stars" represent man's perceptive faculties, including his ability to perceive weight, size, color, sound, and the like. Through concentrating any one of the faculties ("stars") at its focalizing point one may come into an understanding of its action.

17. And God set them in the firmament of heaven to give light upon the earth.

Divine Mind first images the idea, then perceives its fulfillment. Man, co-operating with Divine Mind, places himself under the same creative law and brings into manifestation his ideas.

18. And to rule over the day and over the night, and to divide the light from the darkness: and God saw that it was good.

The idea is the directing and controlling power. Every idea has a specific function to perform. When our ideas are constructive and harmonious we *see* that they are good and realize that their power to rule is dominant in consciousness.

19. And there was evening and there was morning, a fourth day.

"Evening" stands for the fulfillment of an idea and marks another "day" or degree of unfoldment in consciousness.

20. And God said, Let the waters swarm with swarms of living creatures, and let birds fly above the earth in the open firmament of heaven.

"Water" represents the unformed substance of
life, always present as a fecundating element in
which ideas ("living creatures") increase and multiply, just as the earth produces a crop when sown
with seed. The "birds" represent the liberated
thoughts or ideas of mind (heaven).

> 21. And God created the great sea-monsters,
> and every living creature that moveth, wherewith
> the waters swarmed, after their kind, and every
> winged bird after its kind: and God saw that it
> was good.

In connection with the body, "water" represents
the fluids of the organism. The "sea-monsters" are
life ideas that swarm in these fluids. Here is pictured Divine Mind creating the original body idea,
as imaged in the 20th verse. In the 2d chapter of
Genesis we shall read of the perfect manifestation
of this idea. Idea, expression, and manifestation are
the steps involved in bringing anything forth under
divine law. The stamp of good is placed upon divine
ideas and their activity in substance.

> 22. And God blessed them, saying, Be fruitful,
> and multiply, and fill the waters in the seas, and
> let birds multiply on the earth.

In the fifth day's creation ideas of discrimination
and judgment are developed. The fishes and fowls
represent ideas of life working in mind, but they
must be properly related to the unformed (seas) and
the formed (earth) worlds of mind. When an individual is well balanced in mind and body, there is

an equalizing force flowing in the consciousness, and harmony is in evidence.

23. And there was evening and there was morning, a fifth day.

Another orderly degree of mind unfoldment is fulfilled. Another step in spiritual growth is worked out in individual consciousness, when the individual enters into the quickening of his judgment and seeks to conform his ideas to those of Divine Mind.

24. And God said, Let the earth bring forth living creatures after their kind, cattle, and creeping things, and beasts of the earth after their kind: and it was so.

On the sixth day of creation ideas of life are set into activity. "Cattle" represent ideas of strength established in substance. "Creeping things" represent ideas of life that are more subtle in their expression, approaching closer to the realm of sense. They are the micro-organisms. The "beasts" stand for the free energies of life that relate themselves to sensation. Divine ideas are always instantly set into activity: "and it was so."

25. And God made the beasts of the earth after their kind, and the cattle after their kind, and everything that creepeth upon the ground after its kind: and God saw that it was good.

Underlying all these ideas related to sensation, which in their original purity are simply ideas of life functioning in substance, is the divine idea of life. When life is expressed in divine order it is pro-

nounced good. What is termed "sense consciousness" in man is not to be condemned but lifted up to
its rightful place. "As Moses lifted up the serpent
in the wilderness, even so must the Son of man be
lifted up; that whosoever believeth may in him have
eternal life." When the ideas of life are properly
related to love and wisdom, man will find in them
eternal satisfaction instead of sense pleasure.

> 26. And God said, Let us make man in our
> image, after our likeness: and let them have do-
> minion over the fish of the sea, and over the birds
> of the heavens, and over the cattle, and over all the
> earth, and over every creeping thing that creepeth
> upon the earth.

Wisdom and love are the two qualities of Being
that, communing together, declare, "Let us make
man in our image, after our likeness." This is the
mental image of man which in Truth we call the
Christ. The Christ man has dominion over every
idea emanating from Divine Mind.

> 27. And God created man in his own image,
> in the image of God created he him; male and
> female created he them.

Mental activity in Divine Mind presents two
phases: first, conception of the idea; and secondly,
expression of the idea. In every idea conceived in
mind there is first the quickening spirit of life, followed by the increase of the idea in substance. Wisdom is the "male" or expressive side of Being, while
love is the "female" or receptive side of Being.

Wisdom is the father quality of God and love is the mother quality. In every idea there exists these two qualities of mind, which unite in order to increase and bring forth under divine law.

> 28. And God blessed them: and God said unto them, Be fruitful, and multiply, and replenish the earth, and subdue it; and have dominion over the fish of the sea, and over the birds of the heavens, and over every living thing that moveth upon the earth.

Divine Mind blessed the union of wisdom and love and pronounced upon them the increase of Spirit. When wisdom and love are unified in the individual consciousness, man is a master of ideas and brings forth under the original creative law.

> 29. And God said, Behold, I have given you every herb yielding seed, which is upon the face of all the earth, and every tree, in which is the fruit of a tree yielding seed; to you it shall be for food.

"Seed" represents fundamental ideas having within themselves reproductive capacities. Every idea is a seed which, sown in the substance of mind, becomes the real food upon which man is nourished. Man has access to the seed ideas of Divine Mind, and through prayer and meditation he quickens and appropriates the substance of those ideas, which were originally planted in his I AM by the parent mind.

> 30. And to every beast of the earth, and to every bird of the heavens, and to everything that creepeth upon the earth, wherein there is life, *I have given* every green herb for food: and it was so.

Provision is made for the sustenance of all the
ideas emanating from Divine Mind. The primitive
forms of life are fed upon the "herbs," they have a
sustaining force that is food to them, even as the ap-
propriation of divine ideas is food for man.

> 31. And God saw everything that he had made,
> and, behold, it was very good. And there was eve-
> ning and there was morning, the sixth day.

Divine Mind, being All-Good itself, sees only
its own creation as good. As man co-operates
more fully with Divine Mind, imaging only
that which is good, he too beholds his productions
with the "single" eye or sees them only as good.
The sixth step in creation, is the concentration, in
man, of all the ideas of Divine Mind. Man is given
authority and dominion over all ideas. Thus is completed another degree of mind unfoldment.

In the six mind movements, called days, Elohim
God creates the spiritual universe and spiritual man.
He then rests. He has created the ideals, patterns,
for the formed universe that is to follow.

In the next chapter we shall find Jehovah God
executing what Elohim God created or ideated.
In the Hebrew Jehovah means "I am." We identify
Jehovah as the I AM, the spiritual man, the image
and likeness of Elohim God. But spiritual man,
Jehovah, must be clothed upon, so he forms a man
called Adam.

Mysteries of Genesis

CHAPTER TWO

MANIFEST MAN
Study the 2d Chapter of Genesis

Affirmative Prayer

I am inspiring my living substance (Adam) with life and more abundant life, light, and intelligence.

Manifest Man

E SHALL seek to get back of the letter of the Scripture and to discern the spiritual meaning of every passage we consider. With this aim constantly in mind we continue the study of Genesis.

We have seen that the six days of creation in the 1st chapter of Genesis is purely spiritual and ideal. It is plainly stated in the 2d chapter, "There was not a man to till the ground," although the 1st chapter has just described man's creation. This shows that there are two distinct accounts, one of the ideal and only real creation and one of its manifestation. The six days represent six great ideal projections from Divine Mind, reaching a climax in the creation of man. This ideal man, the climax of an ideal creation, is the image and likeness of God, endowed with divine abilities, and possessed of dominion over every idea that Elohim God has projected. The 2d chapter is the story of Jehovah God's *forming*, in manifestation, that which Elohim God had already *created* in mind. This Jehovah God is Christ, spiritual man, or God's perfect idea of man; and He forms the manifest man, who is *I will*, or Adam. The I AM forms and breathes the breath of life into its *I will* creation. In the realm of the ideal we are I AM; expressing those ideals in thought and in act, we are *I will*.

Man is spirit, absolute and unconditioned, but man forms an Adamic consciousness into which he breathes the breath of life. This is the Son of man, called Adam, capable of perfect expression of the divine idea. This Adam is all that we term soul, intellect, and body. We are continually at work with this Adam man, breathing into him or inspiring him with attributes of Being according to our understanding of Truth. Only by infusing into him these sublime ideas can we lift up this son of man and make him the perfect expression of Jehovah, the I AM identity of Elohim.

The divine man created by Elohim, as recorded in the 1st chapter, is male and female, containing within himself both the masculine and the feminine qualities, wisdom and love. These two qualities in union, always produce a third, manifestation. In the creation described in the 2d chapter, when the ideal becomes the manifest man, the woman is separated from man. It is still true, however, that even the manifest man contains within himself both the masculine and the feminine principles. In the subconsciousness of every man is the feminine principle and in that of every woman is the masculine. Much of the unrest and the unhappiness of the human race comes from ignorance of the truth that each individual is both male and female. Men and women search everywhere for some one to give them a feel-

ing of completeness and satisfaction, not knowing
that completion and satisfaction is to be found only
in the spiritual realm of their own being.   The
sense mind interprets the command "Be fruitful,
and multiply, and replenish the earth, and subdue
it; and have dominion" as urging sensual gratification and the physical bringing forth of children.
But it must be remembered that the man to whom
this command was given was a spiritual man not yet
manifest in a physical body.   God creates in mind
and His command is to "be fruitful, and multiply,
and replenish the earth" with true ideas, thoughts,
and words.

After six days of the ideal spiritual creation were
completed by Elohim God there was a period of rest.
"And he rested on the seventh day from all his work
which he had made."   There is a time of relaxation
following a period of concentration, in which the
ideal germinates or prepares itself for coming into
outer manifestation.   The true Sabbath is a state of
mind in which we rest from all concentrated effort
and completely relax.   It is the time when we cease
our daily work of whatever nature and give ourselves
over to quiet contemplation of things spiritual.   It
is an attitude of mind in which we relax the outer
consciousness, let go of all thoughts about material
things and the affairs of daily life in order to enter
into the stillness of spiritual consciousness to think
of God and the fulfillment of His law.   The Sabbath day is kept at any time when we choose to
enter the realm of Spirit to rest from all thought of

temporal things. We let go of "days" because every day is a "Sabbath day" when we retire to rest in the spiritual consciousness.

The name of the first man of the human race is Adam, which means "red" or "ruddy," or "firm," earth. Adam represents generic man, the human race epitomized in an individual-man idea, the first contact of the I AM with life, substance, and intelligence. Eve is the female principle as manifested in generic man.

If the ego that is man faithfully adheres to wisdom and carries out in manifestation the plans ideated in wisdom, there is created a harmonious consciousness, which is symbolized by Adam and Eve in the Garden of Eden.

Adam in his original creation had spiritual illumination. Spirit breathed into him continually the necessary inspiration to give him superior understanding. But he began to "eat" or appropriate ideas of two powers: God and not-God, good and evil. The result of this, as the allegory relates, was that he fell away from his spiritual state of consciousness.

INTERPRETATION OF THE BIBLE TEXT

1. And the heavens and the earth were finished, and all the host of them.

Divine Mind's plans were finished although there was yet no outward manifestation. All is finished first in consciousness and mind then rests, in faith, from further mental activity. This "rest" precedes demonstration.

> 2. And on the seventh day God finished his
> work which he had made; and he rested on the
> seventh day from all his work which he had made.

The seventh day refers to the mind's realization
of fulfillment, its resting in the assurance that all
that has been imaged in it will come forth in expression.

> 3. And God blessed the seventh day, and
> hallowed it; because that in it he rested from all
> his work which God had created and made.

To "hallow" the seventh day is to rest in the
stillness, quiet, and peace of the silence of Mind.
To "hallow" means to keep holy. Holiness is resting in the conviction that there is no lack in the
absolute law that is the law of God. One creates
first in mind by ideating the desired object and then
resting in the assurance that the law of manifestation is being fulfilled.

> 4. These are the generations of the heavens
> and of the earth when they were created, in the day
> that Jehovah God made earth and heaven.

Jehovah, in the Hebrew, is written *Yahweh*.
Yah is the masculine and *weh* the feminine. The
word is made up of masculine and feminine elements and represents the joining together of wisdom
and love as a procreating nucleus. This is the God
who made the visible man, the man of self-consciousness. God manifest in substance is the Jesus
Christ man. Elohim, universal Mind, *creates*, but

Jehovah God *forms.* There is no self-consciousness in
Being, for Being is without beginning or ending.
Universal Mind imaged itself in all that it created,
and all its ideas are contained in the divine-idea
man, which is Jehovah or the Christ.

> 5. And no plant of the field was yet in the
> earth, and no herb of the field had yet sprung up;
> for Jehovah God had not caused it to rain upon the
> earth: and there was not a man to till the ground.

Spiritual creating is ideation in Truth. The
ideas of Divine Mind are contained potentially in
substance, but until these ideas are consciously recognized by Jehovah God, the divine-idea man, they
are not manifest. All things exist as ideas but they
are manifested only as spiritual man becomes conscious of them. The "rain" represents the descent
of ideas into substance. Spiritual man, in whom all
the ideas of Divine Mind are imaged, is not yet
manifest in substance. "There was not a man to till
the ground."

> 6. But there went up a mist from the earth,
> and watered the whole face of the ground.

The "face" represents the outward aspect, while
"ground" stands for formed substance, the product
of related ideas. When man begins to focus his
mind on an objective, there appears at first to be a
"mist" or lack of clear understanding between the
earth consciousness and the spiritual mind. But
this "mist" has its place in the divine economy, for
it "waters" or equalizes the divine radiance.

7. And Jehovah God formed man of the dust
of the ground, and breathed into his nostrils the
breath of life; and man became a living soul.

"Dust" represents the universal substance; it is
that which involves in substance the idea of Divine
Mind, the elemental solution, "waste and void."
"Ground" represents ideal shape or form and corresponds to the "earth" mentioned in the 1st chapter of Genesis. "Dust" represents the radiant earth
or substance. When man (I AM) enters into this
"dust of the ground" (substance) and makes use
of the God ideas inherent in him, he brings forth
the ideal body in its elemental perfection. The real
body of man is not material but is of the nature of
the "universal-dust" body, which is the divine-
substance body. Therefore the perfect image-and-
likeness man is perfect in body as well as in mind.
We should remember that the first Adam was perfect in his elemental soul and body.

Spiritually, "nostrils" represents openness of
mind. The "breath" is the inner life flow that pul-
sates through the soul. The breathing of the manifest man corresponds to the inspiration of the spiritual man. When any man is inspired with high
ideals, he breathes "into his nostrils the breath of
life." Spiritual inspiration quickens man to a consciousness that he is "a living soul." The soul is
the sum total of consciousness and its great objective is a consciousness of eternal life. Through his
I AM or Jehovah God man enters into the soul realm
and rebreathes into it the truths of Being until

these ideas quicken his consciousness to a response that harmonizes it with the underlying Christ principles. Man, spiritually identified, is Jehovah God, co-operating with Elohim God, divine principle, in bringing a spiritual being, the Christ man, to the consciousness of his divinity.

8. And Jehovah God planted a garden eastward, in Eden; and there he put the man whom he had formed.

The Garden of Eden represents a region of being in which is provided all facilities for the production of the beautiful. As described in Genesis it represents allegorically the elemental life and intelligence placed at the disposal of man, through which he is to evolve a soul and body.

The Garden of Eden also describes, in allegory, the elemental forces named by scientists as composing the invisible, etheric universe that Jesus referred to as the "kingdom of the heavens." It also comprehends the activity of those forces in man's soul and body which, when quickened and regenerated, make him a master of all creation. "The kingdom of God is within you." "East" represents the within as "west" represents the without. Jesus also said, "Ye who have followed me, in the regeneration when the Son of man shall sit on the throne of his glory, ye also shall sit upon twelve thrones, judging the twelve tribes of Israel." In our analysis of the Garden of Eden we consider it as a concentration, in man, of all the ideas of God in the process of unfolding man's soul and body. When man is expressing the ideas of Divine Mind, bringing forth the qualities of Being in divine order, he dwells in Eden, a state of bliss, in a harmonious, productive consciousness containing all possibilities of growth.

9. And out of the ground made Jehovah God to grow every tree that is pleasant to the sight, and good for food; the tree of life also in the midst of the garden, and the tree of the knowledge of good and evil.

"Ground" represents formed substance: ideas of Truth of which man is conscious. The "tree" is the substance connecting mind and body, earth and heaven, represented physically by the nerves. The "tree that is pleasant to the sight" portrays the pleasure sensed by ascending and descending currents of life. The substance of spiritual thought is the "food" that is good. The "tree of life also in the midst of the garden" represents the absolute-life principle established in the man consciousness by Divine Mind, the very center of his being. The roots of the "tree of life" are centered in the solar-plexus region and they are symbolized in the physical organism by the nerves of that plexus.

The "tree of the knowledge of good and evil" represents the discerning capacity of mind. Man perceives Truth and then must discern the relation of ideas to Truth before perfect activity is set up.

10. And a river went out of Eden to water the garden; and from thence it was parted, and became four heads.

"River" symbolizes the activity of life in the trees or the current of life in the organism (garden). The "head" of the river represents its directive power.

> 11, 12. The name of the first is Pishon: that is it which compasseth the whole land of Havilah, where there is gold; and the gold of that land is good: there is bdellium and the onyx stone.

Pishon is variously defined as "fully diffused," "real existence," "perfect substantiality," "being carried to its highest degree." Spiritually interpreted, this definition is descriptive of Spirit at work in man's consciousness, Spirit diffusing its ideas of intelligence and light into man's soul. However, this work of Spirit is not confined to man's body or to the earth but is everywhere present. It is the activity of divine ideas in their fullness.

The river Pishon is described as encompassing "the whole land of Havilah." Havilah represents the struggle of elemental life, virtue born of trial, travail, or suffering. There is gold in this land and also precious stones, which means that it is the realm of reality. In other words, we have locked up in our elemental body all the treasures of Spirit. All the precious things of life for which we have been looking are in our body, and it is through the inflow of this mighty spiritual Pishon that these precious ideas are released. But there is a struggle or, as Jesus said, "tribulation" between the spiritual and the natural.

13. And the name of the second river is
Gihon: the same is it that compasseth the whole
land of Cush.

Gihon means variously "formative movement,"
"a bursting forth," "whirlpool," "rapid stream."
This river represents the deific breath of God inspiring man and at the same time purifying his
blood in the lungs. Job said that "there is a spirit
in man," and that "the breath of the Almighty
giveth them understanding." The river Gihon
"compasseth the whole land of Cush." Cush means
"firelike," "darkness," "impurity"; and the passage
refers to the blood-purifying process of the breath.
God is breathing His breath through man's being,
cleansing the blood stream, and filling his whole
being with spiritual inspiration.

14. And the name of the third river is Hiddekel: that is it which goeth in front of Assyria.
And the fourth river is the Euphrates.

Hiddekel means "universal generative fluid,"
"rapid stream," "rapid spiritual influx." The river
Hiddekel symbolizes the spiritual nerve fluid that
God is propelling throughout man's whole being
continually, as the electro-magnetic center of every
physically expressed atom and cell. This wonderful
stream of nerve fluid finds its way over all the many
nerves in man's body temple, giving him the in-
vigorating, steadying power of the Holy Spirit.

Assyria represents the psychic realm or the soul.
The nerve fluid, the most attenuated and volatile

fluid of the body, breaks into flares at the ends of the nerves, giving rise to various kinds of psychical and mental action, forming character or soul. The mind uses the nerve flares to express its ideas.

The fourth river, Euphrates, means "fructify-ing," or "that which is the fructifying cause." Metaphysically, it represents the blood stream. The circulatory system receives and distributes the nu-trients contained in the food we eat. The blood stream is charged with the food substance for bone, muscle, brain, teeth, and hair. Every part of the organism is supplied with substance through this wonderful river Euphrates.

> 15. And Jehovah God took the man, and put him into the garden of Eden to dress it and to keep it.

The Garden of Eden symbolizes the omnipresent, unseen realm out of which comes the visible uni-verse. Modern science has named it the cosmic ether; Jesus called it "the kingdom of the heavens" and Paradise. It cannot be described in human lan-guage, because it transcends all the comparisons of earth. Jesus said that the "mysteries" of the king-dom were revealed to those who were spiritually awake but to others must be told in parables.

The human body with its psychical and spiritual attributes comprises a miniature Garden of Eden, and when man develops spiritual insight and in thought, word, and act voluntarily co-operates with the divine law, then rulership, authority, and dominion become his in both mind and body. "The kingdom of God is within you."

Jehovah God, the active representative of Divine Mind in man, places man in the Garden of Eden to "dress it and to keep it." Man dresses and keeps this garden by developing, in his consciousness, the original, pure ideas of Divine Mind. As man establishes ideas of Truth in his mind he calls into manifestation his spiritual body imaged in sub-stance by Divine Mind.

> 16, 17. And Jehovah God commanded the man, saying, Of every tree of the garden thou may-est freely eat: but of the tree of the knowledge of good and evil, thou shalt not eat of it: for in the day that thou eatest thereof thou shalt surely die.

"Tree" represents the connecting link between the formed substance (earth) and the formless (heaven). To "eat" is to appropriate the substance of ideas through thinking upon them. "Evil" represents the realm of reaction, which is that phase of consciousness which loses sight of the source of all ideas and becomes enamored of the thing formed. Form has its place in creation, but it is subject to the creative idea that begets it. The activity of an idea in mind produces sensation. To become involved in the sensation of an idea to the exclusion of control is to eat of the "tree of the knowledge of good and evil" and die to all consciousness of the original idea.

Materiality as the adverse of spirituality was set up when man became involved in thoughts of the external, in sensation, and lost sight of the creative idea. Because of this, man gradually became separated from the realm of divine ideas; in other words, from God. Death is the result of this separation from God life. Jesus restored the broken life current between God and man and thereby became the "Savior" for those who follow Him.

> 18. And Jehovah God said, It is not good that the man should be alone; I will make a help meet for him.

Man must have avenues through which to express himself. These avenues are the "helpmeets" designed by Jehovah God. Man represents wisdom. It is not good for wisdom to act alone; it must be joined with love in order that harmony may be brought forth. Both the soul and the body are helpmeets to man (spirit), avenues through which he expresses the ideas of Mind.

> 19, 20. And out of the ground Jehovah God formed every beast of the field, and every bird of the heavens; and brought them unto the man to see what he would call them; and whatsoever the man called every living creature, that was the name thereof. And the man gave names to all cattle, and to the birds of the heavens, and to every beast of the field; but for man there was not found a help meet for him.

It is in the soul or substance side of consciousness that ideas are identified, that is, "named." Whatever we recognize a thing to be, that it becomes to us because of the naming power vested in man (wisdom). "Every beast of the field" and the "cattle" represent ideas of strength, power, vitality, and life. These ideas must be recognized by the I AM before they can be formed. "Every bird of the heavens" represents a free thought, and the interchange between the subconscious and the conscious activities of mind. Man has power to name all ideas that are presented to his conscious mind, whether they come from the inner consciousness or from the without.

Wisdom, the masculine of man, needs a helpmeet or balance. Love in the soul (woman) has not yet been developed and established in substance.

> 21. And Jehovah God caused a deep sleep to fall upon the man, and he slept; and he tok one of his ribs, and closed up the flesh instead thereof.

"And Jehovah God [a limited concept of Elohim, the Almighty] caused a deep sleep [mesmeric state] to fall upon the man [Adam]." Nowhere in Scripture is there any record to show that Adam was ever awakened; and he (man) is still in this dreamy state of consciousness. In this dream he creates a world of his own and peoples it with ideas, dimly alive, corresponding to his own sleep-benumbed consciousness.

Paul said, "As in Adam all die [fall asleep, lose spiritual consciousness], so also in Christ shall all be made alive [awaken from coma or lethargy into the awareness of Spirit life]."

Awakening cannot be associated with dying.

The idea that man awakens to spiritual or any kind of consciousness immediately after "death," whether in heaven, hell, purgatory, or elsewhere, is opposed to all reason. His awakening must take place here. during the time of "life," at least while he is partially awake, and before he sinks into that deeper sleep or coma that we call death.

The Scripture admonishes us: "Awake, thou that sleepest, and arise from the dead [the mortal dream of life], and Christ [Truth] shall shine upon thee." David, sensing this truth, said, "I shall be satisfied, when I awake, with thy likeness."

The soul is here coming into the positive development of divine love (the woman). Love is the negative quality of mind and before it can be brought forth, man must enter into the negative side of Being and cease from outer mental activity. This state is symbolized by "deep sleep," sleep being a negative idea. The twelve pairs of ribs represent the externalized expression of the positive and the negative poles of being. When the poles of being are harmoniously adjusted, the positive blend is a new creation. The positive quality is wisdom, the father principle, while the negative quality is love, the mother principle.

22. And the rib, which Jehovah God had taken from the man, made he a woman, and brought her unto the man.

The rib symbolizes the focalizing point of procreation, where the positive and negative qualities

of mind blend as one. Love is brought forth in the
soul in perfect relation to Divine Mind. When man
becomes conscious of himself as a spiritual being,
knowing himself to be the Christ of God, he is I AM
and ready to recreate his world.

> 23. And the man said, This is now bone of
> my bones, and flesh of my flesh: she shall be called
> Woman, because she was taken out of Man.

Wisdom (the man) delights itself in that which
it fathers and procreates. That which is manifest
partakes of the nature of the idea that produced it.
Man and woman are one in spirit, being manifestations of the Father-Mother principle in Divine Mind.

> 24. Therefore shall a man leave his father and
> his mother, and shall cleave unto his wife: and
> they shall be one flesh.

Wisdom and love are the procreating nucleus
of every idea. When an idea has been established in
consciousness we "cleave unto" it, are strongly at-
tached to it. As a result the idea becomes manifest as the substance of our bones and flesh. Man's
body is the "flesh" of his ideas.

> 25. And they were both naked, the man and
> his wife, and were not ashamed.

Wisdom and love are one, inseparable, and not
ashamed. That which is eternally joined as one in
Spirit is not adulterated. Shame comes from adul-
teration.

Mysteries of Genesis

CHAPTER THREE

THE FALL OF MAN

Study: Genesis, chapters 3 and 4.

Affirmative Prayer

I willingly surrender all the claims of sense and follow the commands of Spirit. So I return to the conscious- ness of my original purity and perfec- tion and abide in the garden with Jesus Christ.

The Fall of Man

HE 3D CHAPTER of Genesis is one of the most profound in the Scriptures. It describes in allegory the transgression of the divine law that leads to the negative condition called evil.

The object of creation is to form the formless. Form is the formless projected into self-consciousness. Form implies certain limitations and requires the presence of conditions to sustain its character. The limitations imposed upon form by this need of support must be understood and sustained by the form itself. Hence man must co-operate with God in carrying out the design of creation. Form is established in the first place and its relation to the divine source is sustained by a positive state of mind. This also implies a negative state of mind, the "Adversary."

The serpent was a creation of Jehovah God, "more subtle than any beast of the field." Metaphysically, the serpent represents the life center or generative function, which is not evil when kept in obedience to law. The "woman" is the heart center or love nature. The "garden" is the earthly consciousness and the "tree" is the connection between the earthly and the heavenly consciousness. In the body of man this connecting link is the nervous system and the "fruit" of this tree is the reserve energy, having within it the life giving, fructifying spirit of Being itself.

Man's primary work in the earthly consciousness ("garden") is to use his creative powers to preserve order and harmony in his body and to conserve and use these powers under divine direction. He is put into the garden "to dress it and to keep it," and only when he has done this can he rightfully eat of its fruit. The fruit of that tree, reserve energy, "in the midst of the garden," is to remain inviolate.

The serpent ("Satan") is sensation suggesting to the soul an indulgence in its pleasure beyond the limit of the law fixed by creative Mind. When the soul lets sensation rule its action, the reserve energy is drawn upon, and the connection between the spiritual consciousness and the physical is broken. This causes man to lose his spiritual connection and in that sense he is "lost." It causes him to fall or descend into the lower consciousness of sense, and this is his "fall."

Sense consciousness has involved both the intellect and the heart (man and woman) in a world of false relations. The separation between the body and the spiritual mind has made great havoc in our race harmony. The soul was meant to be the helpmeet of the intellect in keeping the garden of sense consciousness pruned and in perfect order and harmony. To minister to the selfish desires of man is

not the office of the soul. Man was to have dominion over all the works of God and his creative power
was to be exercised in the realm of mind and the
higher soul forces rather than in the purely physical
field.

The body falls to pieces because we are trying,
age after age, to create after the wisdom of Satan
instead of the wisdom of God.

The argument of sense or Satan that through the
knowledge of good and evil man becomes as God
and has his eyes or perceptions opened is altogether
fallacious. The power of the mind to discriminate,
to maintain balanced judgment, comes not from
knowing both good and evil but from knowing good
so unerringly that it can never by any chance be mis-
taken for evil. Man grows in understanding not
through his recognition of opposites but in spite of
such recognition. If it were true that a knowledge
of both good and evil is necessary to true wisdom,
Jesus would not have taught His disciples to pray,
"Deliver us from the evil one." The necessity for
man's deliverance from evil through the action of a
higher consciousness is absolute proof that there is
no connection between true wisdom and the knowledge of evil.

This brings us to a point where we should see
that desire, through listening to sensation, consumes
and wastes the fruit of the tree in the midst of the
garden. This waste is followed by a sense of lack of
vitality. The divine, positive attitude of mind becomes less positive, the consciousness leaves the cen-

ter, the "tree of life," by its nerve branches and takes up its abode in the earthly flesh at the negative circumference. Then it gradually loses its connection with the Divine Mind of God and comes into contact with the negative: it knows both good and evil. Being closer to the negative, it finally loses its hold altogether and is cast out of the garden.

A hint to the wise is sufficient. One phase of the great sin against the law of Being is the misuse of the sexual function. Through misuse we deplete our vitality and waste the elixir of life.

The return to the Garden of Eden, the consciousness of the body in its original purity, is through the "east" or invisible side. "Knock, and it shall be opened unto you." Jesus Christ made the union in His body, re-established the connection between the consciousness in the top brain and the life center that had been broken by the Adamic man. By following His methods and identifying ourselves with His consciousness we also may get back into our former spiritual estate and dwell in the Garden of Eden. "As in Adam all die, so also in Christ shall all be made alive."

Perhaps the "fall of man" may be made a little clearer to the understanding if we consider it in the light of the law of cause and effect. God is the one cause. The fall came about through losing sight of the one great causing Mind. Man became confused and lost in a maze of effects and secondary causes, and this was his fall. The curse that was pronounced upon him was merely the statement of

the law that works innately in Being. If man had
continued to live in the consciousness of his own
Godlikeness, he would have expressed only harmony. Being one with the great causing Mind, he
would himself have caused only harmonious ex-
pressions of life. But he got away from the center
and began to use his formative powers in the realm
of effects, mistaking effects for causes. This produced the many discords that the race experiences.

But with the "curse" there was the promise of
restoration. Bible history concerns itself entirely
with the working out of God's plan of redemption
for humanity. The Spirit of truth is today reveal-
ing to men the truth of their being, and they are
coming to understand that they are made in the
image and likeness of God. Jesus came to show the
way back to the Father, and all those who are letting
go of mortal ignorance and error and conforming
themselves to the perfect Christ mind indwelling are
bringing forth the fruits of righteousness, peace, and
wholeness. To them the promise is now being fulfilled.

INTERPRETATION OF GENESIS 3

1. Now the serpent was more subtle than any
beast of the field which Jehovah God had made.
And he said unto the woman, Yea, hath God said,
Ye shall not eat of any tree of the garden?

The serpent is sense consciousness. It may also
be called desire, sensation, or the activity of life in
external expression apart from the divine source of
life. "Woman" represents love or feeling in the

individual consciousness and symbolizes the soul. Desire for sensation or activity of life in the external first tempts the soul, the center of feeling and emotions. The temptation of sense is at first very subtle, entering the consciousness to stir up doubt, slyly asking the question "Why not?"

> 2, 3. And the woman said unto the serpent, Of the fruit of the trees of the garden we may eat: but of the fruit of the tree which is in the midst of the garden, God hath said, Ye shall not eat of it, neither shall ye touch it, lest ye die.

From the center of one's being the life-giving, ever-bearing tree of the Spirit of God spreads its branches into every department of mind and body. Its fruits are intelligence to the mind, substance to the body, and life to the entire being. The warning given by Jehovah God was that man should not eat of (appropriate) the fruit of this tree. In spiritual revelation we discern that man's cardinal mistake is in appropriating the pure essence of God in order to experience sensuous, selfish pleasure.

> 4, 5. And the serpent said unto the woman, Ye shall not surely die: for God doth know that in the day ye eat thereof, then your eyes shall be opened, and ye shall be as God, knowing good and evil.

The serpent is slyly suggesting to the soul that it indulge in the pleasures of sense and that the experience will result in a deeper understanding of God and His laws. The individual can always find arguments that justify his indulgence to his own mind. This tendency is sensation beguiling man from his

Garden of Eden consciousness.

> 6. And when the woman saw that the tree was
> good for food, and that it was a delight to the eyes,
> and that the tree was to be desired to make one wise,
> she took of the fruit thereof, and did eat; and she
> gave also unto her husband with her, and he did eat.

The woman, the intuitive or feeling side of man's nature, discerns that activity in ideas begets knowledge, but the knowledge gained is not necessarily of a divine nature. Love or feeling (woman) acting independently of wisdom (man) is not reliable.

The "eyes" are the perceptive faculty of mind, and unless the perception is established in Truth one sees or perceives duality. When one delights in knowledge that is less than Truth, the capacity to receive inspiration direct from Divine Mind is lessened or lost. Both love (woman) and wisdom (man) become involved in a counterfeit knowledge through eating (appropriating) ideas inferior to those pertaining to the divine nature.

> 7. And the eyes of them both were opened,
> and they knew that they were naked; and they sewed
> fig-leaves together, and made themselves aprons.

In the Scriptures figs are representative of the "seed" of man. This seed is in its original essence mind energy, and when ideas are related purely to Divine Mind, the seed of man is the life stream in its original purity. Man's sin is the misappropriation of ideas, which leads to sensation. When man and woman are joined—that is, one in sin—they are unclothed of the garment of Truth or "naked."

When wisdom and love, or man and woman, are joined in the consciousness that all their thoughts and acts are inspired by God, the gross sensations of the flesh will be "lifted up," that is, glorified. "I, if I be lifted up, will draw all unto myself."

> 8. And they heard the voice of Jehovah God walking in the garden in the cool of the day: and the man and his wife hid themselves from the presence of Jehovah God amongst the trees of the garden.

The "cool of the day" represents the relaxation or emptiness that follows sense expression. After the high tide of sensation has subsided, the voice of Jehovah God, commonly called conscience, is heard. Man is convinced that he has acted out of harmony with divine law. After experiencing sensation the picture visualized by the conscious mind is impressed upon the life stream and sets up a subconscious tendency. Consciousness would hide from facing this situation, taking refuge amongst the "trees of the garden" (other sensations), but this is not the way to redemption. Every idea is to be handled. All error is forgiven when Truth is brought to bear upon it, and if this method is pursued, only constructive thought habits will be set into activity in the subconscious realm of mind.

> 9, 10. And Jehovah God called unto the man, and said unto him, Where art thou? And he said, I heard thy voice in the garden, and I was afraid, because I was naked; and I hid myself.

Jehovah God walks continually in the garden

(the body) calling unto Adam (life), and when man raises his thoughts and feelings Godward, he contacts the inspiration of Being and builds again the immortal consciousness.

> 11, 12. And he said, Who told thee that thou wast naked? Hast thou eaten of the tree, whereof I commanded thee that thou shouldest not eat? And the man said, The woman whom thou gavest to be with me, she gave me of the tree, and I did eat.

The soul or feminine is the "woman" of man. It is through the affections (love) that man becomes involved in sensation. When a desire of the soul (woman) presses for attention, man often gives way to his feelings instead of raising them, through wisdom, to conform to higher principles.

In Truth feeling must be disciplined and refined and desire for sense pleasures eliminated. When consciousness is purified through the knowledge of Truth and thought force is established in harmonious relation to divine ideas, the woman (feeling) will be joined with man (wisdom) and the holy marriage (generation of divine ideas) will again be brought to light. Celibacy and asceticism have no place in God's plan for man. "For this cause shall a man leave his father and mother, and shall cleave to his wife; and the two shall become one flesh," is written in Genesis and verified by Jesus Christ in Matt. 19:5. Indescribable joy is the heritage of those who submit their sex relations to God in prayer.

> 13. And Jehovah God said unto the woman,

What is this thou hast done? And the woman said,
The serpent beguiled me, and I did eat.

Man, ever seeking excuse for sin, puts the blame
upon God for endowing him with sensation. Sensation is itself a divine creation, and all God's creation was pronounced "good." This brings us to the
root cause of the appetite that craves stimulants and
goes to excess in seeking satisfaction. Through listening to the serpent of sense man goes beyond the
limit set by law natural or divine and becomes a
glutton and drunkard of sensation. The remedy is
to take up the problem from a spiritual standpoint
in the knowledge that sensation is a mental quality
and can be satisfied only by cultivating the spiritual
side of man's nature.

14. And Jehovah God said unto the serpent,
Because thou hast done this, cursed art thou above
all cattle, and above every beast of the field; upon
thy belly shalt thou go, and dust shalt thou eat all
the days of thy life.

When the desire for sensation leads man to dis-
sipate the precious fruit of the tree of life in his
earthly garden, the whole nervous system is depleted
and loses its capacity to contact the higher life current and super-mind wisdom. Then man feels a lack
of something; he is "naked." Sensation is no longer
a heavenly ecstasy but a fleshly vibration, and crawls
upon its "belly," eating "dust" all the days of its life.

16. Unto the woman he said, I will greatly
multiply thy pain and thy conception; in pain thou

shalt bring forth children; and thy desire shall be
to thy husband, and he shall rule over thee.

Instead of bringing forth ideas in the realm of
supersubstance, the feminine is compelled to clothe
her ideas with flesh and bring them forth in the
earthly consciousness.

Having lost consciousness of God as its guiding
light the soul turns to its highest concept of wisdom,
the husband or personal intellect.

17, 18, 19. And unto Adam he said, Because
thou hast hearkened unto the voice of thy wife, and
hast eaten of the tree, of which I commanded thee,
saying, Thou shalt not eat of it: cursed is the ground
for thy sake; in toil shalt thou eat of it all the days
of thy life; thorns also and thistles shall it bring
forth to thee; and thou shalt eat the herb of the
field; in the sweat of thy face shalt thou eat bread,
till thou return unto the ground; for out of it wast
thou taken: for dust thou art, and unto dust shalt
thou return.

The intellect having lost contact with its inner
light is no longer inspired with the ability to idealize
direct from the ether what man needs and is
forced to cultivate the ground and toil physically.
Jesus demonstrated man's spiritual ability when He
produced direct from the ether fishes and loaves to
feed more than five thousand persons.

20. And the man called his wife's name Eve;
because she was the mother of all living.

"Eve" represents love or feeling in individual
consciousness. The I AM (wisdom) puts feeling

into what he thinks and thus Eve (feeling) becomes the "mother of all living." Feeling is the spirit that quickeneth. Woman represents the soul region of Adamic man and the mother principle of God in expression. Back of the woman (feeling) is the pure life essence of God. "Adam" and "Eve" represent the I AM identified in one primal being. They are the primal elemental forces of Being itself.

21. And Jehovah God made for Adam and for his wife coats of skins, and clothed them.

Man was originally connected with the spiritual-body idea, but when he took on personal consciousness, he was given a "coat of skins" under the law corresponding to the quality of his thought world. The "coat of skins" is the body of flesh. When spiritual thought becomes supreme in consciousness, the "coat of skins" will give way to the manifestation of the spiritual body spoken of by Paul. Corruptible flesh is the manifestation of corrupt ideas in mind. "Be ye transformed [changed in form] by the renewing of your mind."

22. And Jehovah God said, Behold, the man is become as one of us, to know good and evil; and now, lest he put forth his hand, and take also of the tree of life, and eat, and live for ever—

"Jehovah God" is written *Yahweh* in the Hebrew, *Yah* being masculine and *weh* feminine. "Jehovah God" is Divine Mind identified as the Christ mind or I AM man. "Good and evil," primarily representing the two poles of Being, are opposite but not adverse to each other. Man developed divine consciousness—came into an understanding of ideas in their relation to Being itself—and when he became involved so intensely in the feeling or negative side of his nature, he lost consciousness of the equilibrium of the Christ mind. Will became independent of wisdom, and an unbalanced condition in both mind and body was set up. And "lest he put forth his hand [appropriating power of mind], and take also of the tree of life, and eat, and live for ever," using the forces of Being toward the expression of a consciousness adverse to the Christ mind, omnipresent wisdom closed the door to the within until man should again enter into the garden by establishing the divine consciousness, Christ, the Way.

23. Therefore Jehovah God sent him forth from the garden of Eden, to till the ground from whence he was taken.

The "garden" symbolizes the spiritual body in which man dwells when he brings forth thoughts after the pattern of the original divine ideas. This "garden" is the substance of God: "Eden," a state of perfect relation of ideas of Being. The "garden of Eden" is the divine consciousness. Having developed a consciousness apart from his divine nature, man must "till the ground from whence he was taken"—that is, come into the realization of God as the substance of his being—and express ideas in harmony with Divine Mind. Wisdom and love are joined in God, and a perfect balance is struck in consciousness between knowing and feeling when man spiritualizes his thoughts.

> 24. So he drove out the man; and he placed at the east of the garden of Eden the Cherubim, and the flame of a sword which turned every way, to keep the way of the tree of life.

The "east" is the within. "Cherubim" refers to protection of the sacred life. The inner spiritual life is protected from the outer, coarser consciousness. The "flame of a sword" is the divine idea or Word of God. Man unites with the inner Word or sacred life through the Christ mind.

INTERPRETATION OF GENESIS 4

The story of Cain and Abel is an allegory of the movement of certain departments of the soul. Cain means "possession." This refers directly to that part of human consciousness which strives to acquire and possess selfishly. Cain was a tiller of the soil, which shows him as of the earthly domain. Abel means "breath," which places him in the air or spiritual realm. The two are brothers; that is, closely related in the consciousness. Abel does not represent the high spiritual consciousness but the life energy that controls the animal functions: he was a sheep raiser. The Hindu metaphysics would call Abel the animal soul and Cain the physical body. Paul would call Abel the "creature" and Cain "the flesh."

Making sacrifices unto Jehovah is symbolic of a refining process that is constantly going on in con-

sciousness. Every thought and act of man sets free
an energy that by the law of attraction proceeds to
its appointed place in the various realms of mind
and body. Jehovah is the one universal Mind, which
is the receptacle of all thoughts and receives all.
When you have a thought of love and good will,
you set free invisible emanations that are impreg-
nated with those ideas. These ascend to a higher
realm and form a part of your spiritual soul, at the
same time relating you to Jehovah, who is the presiding oversoul of the race. This is the inner meaning of the offering of sacrifices to Jehovah.

Everything in nature is going through this refining process, and there is a constant ascension of substance to mind and of mind to Spirit. We are taught
that a period will finally come when the whole universe will be resolved back into its original essence
in God.

The thoughts of the mind are nearer to the
Spirit than are the emanations of the body. Hence
the offering of Abel (mind) was more acceptable
to Jehovah than was that of Cain (body). The
killing out of all human sympathy and love by the
body selfishness is the slaying of Abel by Cain.
When the body demands possession of all the resources of mind and soul, it reduces existence to
mere material living; it has slain Abel, whose blood
of life then cries from the earthly consciousness
(ground) to Jehovah for expression.

When the selfishness of the body has killed out
the finer impulses of the soul and reduced all the

higher aspirations to a material level of existence, there is no longer any pleasure in living. Without the soul the body is a mere machine with little sensation, that makes no progress. Cain thus tills the ground but it yields him no strength.

The body feels its degradation, and those who get into this degenerate condition are usually miserable. Thus Cain's punishment is great. He fears the vengeance of the other faculties; fears that they may condemn the body (Cain) for its impotency. But Jehovah, divine law, has fixed a limit to this condemnation, and we are warned that we must not destroy the body, however great its sins. This mark set upon Cain to prevent his being slain, is the consciousness of his divine origin. No matter how deep the body ego may be in transgressions, it still bears the stamp of God and can never be killed out entirely. We cannot kill life, for it is eternal, but we can allow the body ego (Cain) to kill the consciousness of life within the individual organism. The third son of Adam and Eve, Seth, was born after the death of Abel. The name Seth means "compensation," "substituted," but more particularly it carries the idea of settled, placed, set. The root idea is that of a surrounding, sympathetic movement that envelops a thing and defines its limits; places, bounds, or disposes of it. Some mystics have seen in the name a law of destiny: that which predetermines a thing and settles its order.

While man is in a sense a creature of free will, yet in a larger sense he is a son of God, made in

His image and likeness and destined to express and
demonstrate spiritual perfection. There is in all the
universe, including man, a balancing power of good,
of perfection, that causes readjustment and healing
to set in after every transgression of law or wander-
ing away from that which is wholesome and true.
This is clearly set forth in Bible symbology and history. Every time man has wandered away, gone to
extremes, a reaction has set in and he has been led
back to a saner level. It is thus that he evolves and
grows into a full consciousness of his perfect good.
His growth in Christlikeness is greatly accelerated
however when he comes into a knowledge of the
Truth that makes him free, and begins to think and
act consciously and voluntarily in harmony with it.

Mysteries of Genesis

CHAPTER FOUR

THE REACTION TO SENSE LIVING

Study: Genesis, chapters 6, 7, 8, 9, and 11

Affirmative Prayer

I am a spiritual being, and by faith in the Christ mind within me I rise above the flood of material belief.

The Reaction to Sense Living

THE FLOOD

THERE HAVE been many floods upon the earth and nearly every race has traditions of a time when to them "the whole earth" was engulfed in a great deluge. Geologists are agreed that there have been many deluges in the history of the earth. But these do not necessarily refer to the Flood of Genesis, nor do they corroborate it as history.

As history, the great rain in the Genesis story is very uncertain, and from a historical standpoint we should gain but little of value from its study. But as an idealistic description of certain habits of thought either in the individual or in the race and of the result of those habits of thought in consciousness, we can profit much from its study.

When we observe cloud formations over the earth we can be sure that rain is indicated. The wind may blow the clouds away from the immediate vicinity, but some other part of the earth will get the rain. The downpour may be delayed for hours, even days, but once the clouds have formed the rain will descend sooner or later.

Clouds formed by ignorant or erroneous thinking also indicate a coming storm. The effect of untrue thoughts may become manifest in any part of the body. Manifestation may be delayed for days, years, or even longer periods, but eventually it will come. There is no way to hold it back or to prevent it, but there is a way to escape the effect of it.

The trials and reverses in the life of an individual can be traced to a definite cause in his thinking. There has been some error of belief or some confusion of thought, which in its natural course under the law has worked itself into outer expression as an apparent loss, an accident, a disappointment, or a disease. We deplore the condition, yet see in it two possibilities of good. First the manifestation has fulfilled the law and given an avenue of escape for the pent-up error within, and secondly, it has taught a valuable lesson. There is small comfort in the thought that an earthquake has relieved a strained and abnormal condition in the earth's crust. Yet when we look a little deeper we see that a strained and abnormal condition in the race thought that had to become manifest has been relieved and the race consciousness is the better for it. If all could understand this law of thought expression, we should realize that our thinking not only influences our own affairs but contributes to the total race thought and by the same law comes into expression in the race environment. Spiritually we are much our brother's keeper, his welfare depending upon our true thinking as well as on our social or commercial intercourse with him.

When we lower our ideals to a material basis, "the sons of God" are taking unto themselves wives of "the daughters of men." "Jehovah saw that the wickedness of man was great in the earth, and that every imagination of the thoughts of his heart was only evil continually." When we join spiritual faculties like faith, will, and imagination to the material surroundings, personalities, and sensual desires, we are falling short of the law of Being, which is that these higher faculties shall draw from the formless and be united to that realm. To unite spiritual faculties with the things of sense is in direct opposition to divine law and in the Scripture is termed "wickedness."

When the wrong use of the spiritual faculties reaches a certain limit, the law (Lord) of our being begins to regulate the consciousness. Outraged nature reacts; a destruction of the false, man-made condition sets in. This is the "flood" of Noah which is symbolized in the Book of Genesis.

Lamech, Noah's father, is a name signifying "a strong young man," and the name Noah means "rest." In the days of our youth we idealize the material world and attach our spiritual faculties to the things of sense. This attachment becomes so complete that we no longer use our spiritual faculties for their proper functions on the spiritual plane. This results in abnormal conditions and a balance must be restored. The law of reaction sets in and there is a flood of seemingly adverse experiences. But Noah (rest) finds "grace in the eyes of God."

One who has indulged the strength of youth in the things of sense until the law of spiritual equilibrium begins to work itself out in a rest, may have bodily ills. The error thoughts have brought about a precipitation by crosscurrents in the body consciousness, the wicked or negative thoughts crossing with the spiritually positive ideas. This is followed by the "flood," which drowns out the material thoughts and cleanses the earth. In one sense the Flood typifies that state of consciousness in which the physical is overtaken by the catastrophe of death.

Science teaches that man's body contains all the elements that are found in the earth. This gives rise to the thought "ashes to ashes, dust to dust." Religion however goes a step further and says that man is the epitome of Being, that he is like his Maker in spirit, soul, and body, the image and likeness of God. If man's body is of the same character as the earth, it is in some of its phases like its prototype. The earth's surface is three fourths water and the body is about eighty per cent water. This is a major negative condition that needs but little augmenting to cause an overflow or a flood. It is only our positive spiritual thoughts that hold back a deluge, and once there is an overbalance the negative is let loose and there is great destruction. There is no stopping this flood by any material means, and one who is spiritually wise will not fear it but rather rejoice in the cleansing it brings about.

Just as the earth's waters evaporate and surround it with clouds of mist, so the mists and clouds of life surround man's body. As the electrical forces move upon these mists and clouds of earth, so do the mental forces move upon and cause the invisible ethers to condense and flood the body with its own negative thoughts. The poetic words "A flood of thoughts came o'er me" is no metaphor but a physical fact. When mind and body reach a certain tenseness or strained condition, the law forces a conjunction and a flood is certain to follow. This is shown by what is called "nervous breakdowns." Some one has said that America is fast becoming a nation of neurotics. We certainly need this lesson of Noah ("rest") to learn to let go of physical tenseness and material things. This rest can be attained only when we realize that our faculties are spiritual and must seek spiritual expression.

Man is an epitome of all that exists in Being, even unto the Spirit of God, which is inspired in him. But man is a free agent. He can open his mind to the divine intelligence and know the creative law, or he can work out his character through blind experimentation. Our race is in the experimental stage. In our ignorance we transgress the law to the very limit and a great reaction then sets in. We may name this reaction diabetes or dropsy or what not. Such names express a general condition that is negative to the point of dissolution. Then that in us which always looks obediently to God in extremity is awakened and we seek the divine law. This obedient disposition is Noah, through whom the seed of a new state of consciousness is saved.

The only refuge from this flood is in the ark of Jehovah, which is built by "rest" (Noah) in the spiritual part of us, right in the midst of the flood of error. Noah heeded not the jeers of the people about him but rested upon the promise of God.

Your ark must be built upon a scientific understanding of Truth as to the presence, power, and wisdom of God. This is signified by the mathematical dimensions prescribed to Noah. The ark is built upon affirmations of what you are in Spirit. You take into it your wife, your sons and their wives (spiritual principles inhering in the soul), and "of every living thing of all flesh, two of every sort" (male and female or positive and negative activities of life in the organism).

The idea of divine Truth must be fed with true affirmations as you are being lifted up and above the flood of error thoughts that surge about you. In due time the waters of negation will subside and enable you to walk forth and to people your world with new and better ideas.

The story of Noah and the Flood portrays in wonderful symbolism the manner in which one of the faculties of being operates in unfolding the perfect man. The faculty of renunciation is twofold in action: it eliminates the error, and expands the good. The name Noah symbolizes the sweet rest and quiet comfort that come after the soul has worked out some of its problems in consciousness and has perceived that there is an original spark of divinity in man that is most sacred and holy and that the expansion of this original divine spark is man's spiritual development. Jehovah, the image-and-likeness man created by Elohim God, recognizes only the good and instructs His Adam man to open his consciousness to good thoughts and to cleanse his consciousness from all evil by the flood waters of denial.

Man is making his body temple an eternal dwelling place for the soul. His goal is to bring to expression the kingdom of the heavens and to establish it within himself. To do this he needs to realize that the old is constantly passing away and the new constantly coming in, according to the outworking of the law. He should not resist this change but rather assist in bringing it about. We are born daily and we die daily in some phase of consciousness. Some errors may stick in our mind for a while, but when new light is born in consciousness, old thoughts are carried away by Noah's Flood.

Noah and his three sons represent the mind of the Spirit in us. The sons typify three states of consciousness in every one of us. Ham, meaning "hot," typifies the physical; Japheth, meaning "extended and wide," typifies the intellect or reason; and Shem, meaning "renowned," typifies the spiritual state of consciousness. In Genesis 9:18-28 we see how these sons acted toward their father.

Noah had planted a vineyard, and he drank of the wine or took into his physical nature the juice of the grapes. This is symbolical of the new spiritual life that is still contaminated with the sense consciousness. Noah had given his attention to the cultivation of the vineyard (earth consciousness) rather than the cultivation of the spiritual consciousness. More thoroughly to explain the drunkenness of Noah we must resolve the elements of the allegory into their spiritual ideas.

Noah became uncovered or naked, lost his garment of Truth, by mixing sense (artificial) stimulants with the new wine of life, Spirit. His cultivation of the life force in this physical manner is like the work of some of our physical scientists. Athletes cultivate the physical in an effort to increase the flow of life force, and imagine that the physical side is the whole thing. Instead of illuminating Noah or giving him life the wine put him to sleep. He was intoxicated by error thought and this opened his consciousness to negation. The higher man saw at once that he was not expressing spiritual Truth.

Although the sons of Noah were supposed to be on a higher plane than he, yet they were also in sense consciousness, in a measure, and this especially applied to Ham. Now there is a higher and a lower physical consciousness, and the name of Canaan, Ham's son, is introduced to symbolize the lower physical thought. Ham saw the ignorance and the nakedness that sense thinking had produced in his father but did nothing to remedy it, nor did he try to extenuate the uncovering in any way. To Ham the thing was more or less a joke and he told his brothers about it, evidently in a scandalous way. This reveals that man cannot get spiritual life out of material thought.

Shem, representing the Spirit in man, and Japheth, the intellectual nature, have pity on the exposure of man's nakedness and sensuality and try to cover it up without seeing it as a reality. They put a garment over their shoulders and walked backward and spread it over their father's nakedness. They did not view the occurrence as a reality.

When Noah awoke from his wine, that is, returned to his spiritual consciousness, his first words were "Cursed be Canaan." Canaan means "lowland" and represents the body consciousness. "A servant of servants shall he be unto his brethren," thus placing the stamp of materiality upon the body consciousness and showing that it cannot give spiritual life.

But Noah said to the God of Shem, "Let Canaan be his servant," that is, let the flesh come under the dominion of the spiritual man. Of Japheth Noah said, "Let him dwell in the tents of Shem"; that is, let the intellectual man dwell under the protection of the spiritual man, not as a servant but as a younger brother. Thus the physical man (Ham) and the lower sense consciousness (Canaan) come under the dominion of both the intellectual man and the spiritual man, the I AM itself.

The sons of Noah represent the positive, permanent thoughts that rise above the negative, wicked conditions, even the catastrophe of death (flood), and come down to earth again. In other words, they are carried over and reincarnated when the soul again takes on a body of flesh.

In order to get the most from physical man we must seek to develop him along spiritual lines. When the spiritual man (Noah) begins a new cycle, a new evolution in physical consciousness (after the cleansing of the "flood"), we must give attention to the impact of the ideas put into the body consciousness; select carefully the food and drink; and refuse to give ourselves to the sense consciousness.

In Genesis 9:8-17 we read that God made a covenant with Noah that the earth should not again be flooded, and the rainbow was given as a symbol of this covenant. The rainbow as a token of the covenant between God and the earth involves the law of obedience. It is also symbolic of the human race and of the law of unity. The rainbow is formed of many drops of water, each of which acts as a prism, receiving light from the sun and transmitting it by refraction. Each drop represents a human being and the whole the race. Only as the drops refract the sun's rays do they become visible and only as man "refracts" God does he make his demonstration. The seven colors of the solar spectrum are produced by different rates of vibration of a universal energy, which in its myriad activities makes the visible universe.

When man is like Noah, obedient to the guidance of God, he is never flooded by negative conditions. When the whole race enters into this obedience, the perfect principles of unity and God refraction and reflection will be forever established. The rainbow is the sign of this state in which we shall

all form with our obedient minds a circle of natural perfection. As the rainbow connects the heavens and the earth, so the state of perfect obedience and unity in Spirit will bring the earth and the kingdom of the heavens together as one.

THE TOWER OF BABEL

In the 11th chapter of Genesis is related the building by the descendants of Noah of a city and a tower that was to reach to heaven. "And the whole earth was of one language and one speech," which indicates that there was unity in the interchange of intelligence and purpose but that it was based upon materiality: "And they had brick for stone, and slime had they for mortar." They built the city and the tower, but Jehovah confounded their language and they were scattered abroad "upon the face of all the earth."

Some Bible authorities claim that the word Jehovah in this paragraph meant "chief" in the original Hebrew and should have been so translated. In other words, it was the Adversary or personal ego of the people that asserted its disintegrating nature and destroyed the work of their hands.

Whether the story of the building of Babel and the scattering of its people be history or allegory matters little; it illustrates the ephemeral character of man's work exemplified times beyond number in the buried cities of the past. Not only cities but great nations have occupied large areas of this earth, only to be swept away.

This universal scattering of the nations that bravely set out to build cities and civilizations planned to reach to heaven and endure forever, should make thinking persons pause and inquire the cause of such stupendous failure. The fact is that the foundations of their cities were material instead of spiritual, there was an excess of "stone, and slime."

However, every great nation has claimed God as its originator and often its temporal heads as ruling by divine right. As long as these nations had faith in this divine source they prospered, but when the personal element began to assert itself, decline set in, the nation collapsed, and its people scattered.

This is not only the history of cities and nations but also of numerous colonies of Utopian pattern for the betterment of men. Their plans are perfect and appear to be based upon laws that will work toward universal happiness and prosperity. But they all fail because their leader is some human, and there is always some other human in the colony who is ambitious to rule. Politics and party strife then enter and break down the unity that is so necessary to the success of any enterprise.

History shows that just preceding a great national collapse dictators or "chiefs" assume the power personally to make and enforce the laws for the people. This condition repeats itself in world affairs and always presages a breakdown of man-made civilization. The towers of Babel totter and philosophic onlookers foretell a lapse of the human family into primitive savagery.

That the principles upon which the governments
of the world are based are inadequate to meet the
needs of a world nation is patent to any one who
studies the economic and moral status of various
countries. God created all men of one blood, according to the Scriptures, and that universal bond
of humanity is asserting itself in the tremendous increase in facilities for intercourse among men of
every country. So the struggle for separate national
existence must be broken down and a new and larger
understanding of race solidarity established.

So we see that history is repeating itself on a
larger scale than ever before and is again ready to
scatter the inhabitants of Babel who have attempted
to build to heaven without God. After the break-
ing up of the present materially founded governments, the spiritually wise will get together and form
a federation based upon the principles laid down by
Jesus Christ, and we shall then enter into that universal peace and security called the millenium. "And
this gospel of the kingdom shall be preached in the
whole world for a testimony unto all the nations;
and then shall the end come." The prophecies of
Jesus, as set forth symbolically in Matthew 24, un-
doubtedly point to their fulfillment at this time, and
the "tribulations" there recited are upon us, but we
need not be fearful or troubled if we are depending
upon God to take care of us. "The race is not to
the swift, nor the battle to the strong," "but he that
endureth to the end, the same shall be saved."

Mysteries of Genesis

CHAPTER FIVE

THE INITIAL STEP TOWARD REDEMPTION

Study: Genesis, chapters 12, 13, and 14

Affirmative Prayer

I earnestly desire to enter into the kingdom of God, to do His will, and thus to have all things added unto me.

The Initial Step toward Redemption

THE CALL OF ABRAHAM

THE CALL of Abraham is considered the initial step in a great plan for the redemption of the Adam race from its material, sensual consciousness, called the fall of man. From any mortal viewpoint the time seems long and the way tortuous, but we may, if we will, enter into the mind of the Spirit, where one day is as a thousand years and a thousand years are as one day, and here we see the whole plan worked out in a definite, systematic, and orderly way.

Every detail in Abraham's experience has a definite correspondence in the life of each one who is bringing forth the Christ man. A study of these things is therefore of great importance to all who seek the realization of sonship. To them it is given to understand "the mystery which hath been hid for ages and generations."

Abraham represents faith, the first great faculty developed or "called out" by man in the unfoldment of his spiritual nature or Christ mind. Faith is that faculty by which we know God as omnipresent Spirit substance. This substance is man's supply, as Paul discerned when he said, "Faith is the substance of

76

things hoped for." By faith we appropriate the
spiritual substance of whatever things we desire,
thus taking the first step necessary to their manifestation. Abraham, rich in faith, increased his substance until it was very great.

Volumes might be written about faith in its relation to the conscious, subconscious, and superconscious departments of mind; or about its centers of
action in the body. Abraham represents faith in its
early establishment in consciousness, and his life
portrays the different movements of this faculty on
the various planes of action in man's being. In order
to understand the lessons that Abraham's life has
for us, a certain familiarity with each plane of consciousness is necessary.

That in the individual which is called "I" may be
termed attention. It is in reality the spiritual man.
It is the inherent capacity of the "I" to recognize
ideas, and through the law of Being to form ideas
into states of consciousness. By forming states of
consciousness and setting up action in their various
departments, the "I" (attention) can then leave
them, as the millwright leaves the mill he has con-
structed over a waterfall. Nature carries on the
work once it is established.

So we find ourselves in possession of states of
consciousness that may seem to be ignorant. There
is, for instance, a subconsciousness that carries on
digestion, assimilation, circulation, respiration, elimination, and the like. We could not be in possession
of an organism having these various movements of

mind unless at some point in our experience we had established them. If we consciously assumed these functions ourselves, it is plainly possible that we can again go back of them and become familiar with their subconscious action.

Thus it is a question of attention whether or not we shall know about the various planes of consciousness. If we rivet our attention for but ten minutes a day upon the heart, we shall in a short time know what is going on at that center. So with every department of the organism. Whatever the process being carried on by an organ in the body, you may be assured that a center of consciousness is located somewhere in the vicinity of the organ, and you may by continually centering your attention there become familiar with the office and work of that organ.

Abraham represents man in the first awakening of his faith, when he is dominated by it. The very name has come to be almost a synonym for faith. Abraham was dwelling in a realm of limited thought, and he was called out by Spirit into a great expansion of all his thoughts and powers through faith. All the people and places mentioned in connection with his history have a symbolical meaning. They represent other faculties and phases of mind that are called into expression along with faith.

The movement in consciousness here represented is that of an individual who has been spiritually inactive or laggard. The name of Abraham's father, Terah, signifies "loitering." The Lord or spiritual impulse within, presses forth to religious activity.

It virtually says, "Get thee out of thy country, and from thy kindred, and from thy father's [loiterer's] house, unto the land that I will show thee."

When this call comes, lofty ideas begin to possess the mind. The name in its original form, Abram, means "exalted father." Faith in the unseen God and in divine guidance inspires lofty thoughts that become part of the consciousness without special effort when man is obedient to the call of Spirit. To those who depend upon the evidence of the senses it may be blind faith, but it works out beautifully in the life of those who are true to it.

This lack of understanding of all the resources of God in His Promised Land, however, must necessarily leave voids and waste places in the consciousness. There was a famine in Abram's land and this caused him to go down into Egypt. The name Egypt means the realm of substance and life in the depths of the body consciousness. This is in a sense a region of darkness and mystery, yet a great kingdom, rich in substance and essential to the perpetuation of the body. It refers to the vitality of the abdominal region. Those who are not in an all-round understanding of the divine law do not know how to affirm the flow of a steady current of life from below to feed the flame of intelligence above and therefore have periods of bodily exhaustion. In this state they seem to lose divine guidance and are plunged into apparent darkness (Egypt). This is a very necessary adjustment, however.

Here again we see the result of a lack of spiritual

understanding. Sarah, the wife of Abram, represents the soul, the affectional or emotional part of
man. Her name signifies "princess" and the soul is
indeed the daughter of a king. It should never be
allowed to unite in any way with matter or material
conditions. Not having the divine understanding
when he was drawn down into the vital processes of
the organ of recuperation (Egypt) Abram allowed
his love, affection, and emotion (Sarah) to become
united to the ruling state of mind there (Pharaoh),
and this brought plagues upon the land of Egypt.

It is right and proper to recognize the vital center
in the organism, represented by the generative center, as having its legitimate place in the divine
economy; but man should never become involved in
mere animal sensation. This is what brings the plagues
upon Egypt: or diseases upon the human family.

Metaphysicians who are regenerating their bodies
through the power of their I AM word should heed
this lesson. When quickening, cleansing, and read-
justing the cells at this life center, they should si-
lently declare: *"The sensation of the flesh cannot
hold my love, for my love is the daughter of God,
and we are joined in purity and pure desire in my
Father's house."* Thus shall they escape the plagues
of Egypt and the rebuke of Pharaoh: "What is this
that thou hast done unto me? why didst thou not
tell me that she was thy wife?"

Among others closely associated with Abraham
was Lot, the son of Haran, Abraham's brother.
When Abraham went to seek a new country (con-

sciousness) in response to the call of Spirit, Lot went with him. The name Lot means "hidden," "concealed," "covert," and signifies the negative side of faith. When faith expands in the consciousness, goes out into a new and greater country, its old aspect goes with it and expands also. Lot may also be said to symbolize the part of man's consciousness that is still in darkness; in other words, the natural or animal man. This part of man's nature he cannot escape, but must take with him into the new country. He can however lift it up to his level, as Abraham did, for we read that Lot prospered also.

For a time Abraham pitched his tent at a place midway between Bethel and Ai. He was later to return to this place and become established, after his separation from Lot. Bethel means "house of God" and Ai means "a heap of rubbish." This refers to the establishment in the consciousness of a higher faith, a faith in God. Jesus said, "Have faith in God." This God faith has an established and definite place in man's very body. Bethel refers to the medulla and Ai (eye) to the pineal gland, which is at the very center of the head and resembles a half-opened eye. Anatomists have found grains of sand at the center of this gland (heap of rubbish).

The return from Egypt is symbolical of man's return to spiritual consciousness after his "fall." "Out of Egypt did I call my son" was not a single event; it occurs again and again in the Bible story and is repeated in the case of every individual who comes into a realization of his spiritual identity. The

whole nation of Israel was called out of Egypt to
assume its destiny of bringing forth the fruit unto
righteousness and life everlasting, to play a part in
the restitution of the race to its Edenic state. Jesus
came up out of Egypt where His parents had taken
Him as a child. Abraham, faith, did not remain
long in the darkness of sense consciousness.

Abraham returned out of the land of Egypt, "and
Lot with him"; for the time had not yet come when
Abraham could part with the subjective or psychic
and dwell in the purely spiritual consciousness.

Until the Christ mind is firmly established in the
individual there is a certain residue of faith in negative appearances. This divided state of mind causes
confusion and discord. This is typified by the strife
between the herdsmen of Abraham's cattle and the
herdsmen of Lot. The time comes when by reason
of the increase of faith or substance these two aspects of mind cannot dwell together: "the land was
not able to bear them."

It was Abraham rather than Lot that suggested
the separation. When man reaches a certain point
in his spiritual development he realizes that he must
let go of everything that retards his progress. Lot
is typical of the natural man, always eager to take
the best for himself. He chose the plain of the Jordan because it was "like the land of Egypt."

True faith in God separates itself from all negative belief that the body is material, impure, or
transient. The herdsmen of Abraham were separated from the herdsmen of Lot. So the senses of

the man who has centered his faith on the invisible are by degrees separated from the appeal of his lower nature and become true herdsmen of his enduring thoughts. As a true seer his vision is fixed on the changeless reality inhabiting all form, the substance of which all visible manifestation is but the configuration. His ear becomes attuned to the unbroken harmony of life that is permeating his mind, his body, his soul, and the world about him. He learns so to direct his thought of Spirit substance that one touch of his mind upon the hidden spring opens the way for the healing of the body, if a belief in material imperfection should find lodgment in his consciousness.

When we put our faith wholeheartedly into spiritual reality and follow our ideal without wavering, we are willing to allow sense consciousness the choice of its own field of action. Abraham gave Lot his choice of the land. When we withdraw our interest from the natural man, there is a separation. True thought and untrue thought cannot intermingle.

Canaan means "lowland," but it was here that Abraham lived after his separation from Lot. Is it not significant that this "lowland" became the Promised Land, the land "flowing with milk and honey"? True faith, which works through love, has power to refine the body and so make it the Promised Land of the soul. When man rediscovers this lost domain, the promises of Scripture will be fulfilled.

Every faculty of the mind has an active and a passive side, an objective and a subjective, a positive

and a negative. Abram represents the faculty of
faith in its positive expression. To complete the
symbol we find Lot (hidden, concealed) representing the negative aspect of faith. His domain is the
flesh. He accompanied Abram into Egypt and back
again. When they separated, Lot chose to dwell in
the "Plain of the Jordan . . . like the land of
Egypt, as thou goest unto Zoar." The river Jordan
here symbolizes the descending flow of thought running through the organism from head to foot. When
mortal beliefs rule the individual, the life flow is
muddy with sense concepts and turbulent with materiality. The Jordan is noted as a muddy stream.
Zoar means "smallness," littleness, and represents
that which is inferior. We should beware how we
link our I AM consciousness with the faith that is
established in the flesh, typified by Lot.

Lot and all his possessions were carried away by
Chedorlaomer and the kings with him, who signify
the rule of sensuality in man. These sense beliefs
and desires have seemingly overpowered the negative
phase of faith that Lot symbolizes. The power of
this phase of faith has been taken over to build up
and sustain flesh that is ruled over by carnal thought.
But when knowledge of this occurrence comes to the
positive side of the faith faculty in the individual
(Abram) who has come up out of material thought
(Egypt) and passed to a higher concept of God
(Hebrew), let us see what happens. Positive faith
(Abram) gets into action with a thought power
that destroys sense rule (Chedorlaomer and his al-

lies) and restores negative faith (Lot) to its rightful place in consciousness.

Mamre ("strength"), and Aner ("adolescent youth"), the Amorites who "were confederate with Abram," suggest thoughts of vigor and abundant substance, which were inspired by faith. These thoughts are apparently material in expression (Amorites), yet they are friendly toward the individual's higher concepts or faith in God (Abram), because in reality their true origin is Spirit. They lend their conception of strength and power to the aid of faith while it is gaining its victory over error.

Faith brings into action all its accumulated wisdom and understanding ("he led forth his trained men") and makes a union with the judgment faculty (Dan). Then faith strikes at the very root of sensuality, the mortal man's belief that life is material. This belief is the hiding or lurking place (Hobah) for the error thoughts symbolized by the kings who took Lot captive.

We can never fully overcome sensuality until we put away belief in materiality. We must know that our whole being, including the body, is not material but spiritual. Sowing to the belief in the flesh we reap the corruption of the flesh, but by sowing to Spirit we reap eternal life. (Damascus also, like Hobah, signifies a state of consciousness founded upon a material conception of the life in the body.)

We find a rich symbology in the story of Abram's victorious return from the battle. He was met at the "vale of Shaveh," which means "plain," a level place, a place of equality, by Melchizedek, whose name means "king of righteousness," priest of God, and who here symbolizes the Christ consciousness in the individual. The king of Sodom also met and greeted Abram on the "plain" of equality (Shaveh). He here represents the ruling power in the physical.

When the Christ consciousness rules in both the mind and the body, the individual is established in right thinking and right doing (righteousness). Then he has come to the place of peace, poise, equilibrium, and wholeness signified by Shaveh. When this place is reached in both the inner and the outer consciousness (Salem and Sodom) there is a great increase of substance and of life in one's realization. This increase comes from the higher spiritual mind within, the Christ, and is symbolized by the bread and the wine that Melchizedek gave to Abram. Melchizedek blessed Abram and blessed God, and Abram gave him "a tenth of all." When a person realizes that his victories are gained by the power of God alone, he should willingly use a tenth of his increase of power, understanding, and substance for the furtherance of the Christ Truth.

Abram refused the proffered gifts of the king of Sodom (verses 21 to 23), which teaches us that there must be a lifting up and transmuting of the seemingly material life and substance in the body before it can be utilized by the higher faculties of the mind. None of the credit for the multiplication of substance and strength should be given to the mortal in man. Spirit gives all the increase of good.

Mysteries of Genesis

CHAPTER SIX

THE PROMISE OF SALVATION

Study: Genesis, chapters 15, 16, 17, and 18

Affirmative Prayer

I have the faith of Christ in God's unfailing substance now forming in my mind and becoming manifest in all my affairs.

The Promise of Salvation

GOD'S COVENANT WITH ABRAHAM

FAITH IN things spiritual is not born full orbed and perfect. It has its stages of growth in man. The parable of the mustard seed is applicable in this as in many other instances. Up to the time of Abraham man had no soul consciousness. He had lost that in his fall into sense consciousness. The story of Abraham teaches how the consciousness of soul and of the soul's relation to God again dawns in the race mind, beginning a long period of growth that reaches perfection in the Christ demonstration of Jesus. Therefore Abraham's history and his varied experiences are to be read as relating to the evolution of the soul and not to externality. The early stages of this soul growth are symbolized in the experiences of Abraham, the typical man of faith.

The earliest growths of faith are not deeply rooted. We find Abraham at first living in a tent, which indicates that faith had not yet become an abiding quality in the consciousness of man. Through certain movements of the mind faith takes a firmer hold and finally establishes the "firmament" mentioned in the 1st chapter of Genesis.

Abram and his wife Sarai, as they were called before their names were changed to Abraham and Sarah, were both old and had no children. Symbolizing faith and soul, they were as yet without fruit. Deep within his heart Abram cherished an intense desire for a son as heir to his own growing faith and the perpetuation of his own spiritual vision. This desire was later to test his faith in the reality of the unseen and in the power of Spirit to bring the unseen into visible manifestation.

Not only was Abram to be himself blessed and given a great name but he was to be a blessing to the race in turn. This required something positive of him; namely the establishment of his faith in the invisible good as being present and active, to the exclusion of a negative faith or acceptance of appearances. Thus the promise of God to Abram was not alone a promise to a son to gratify his personal desires; it was a promise that, with a spiritual background to his life, the impossibilities confronting the natural man no longer exist and are to be put out of mind. Abram was the founder of the faith that "with God all things are possible."

Abram's son and the great nation that he was to father were thus first formed in Abram's mind by faith in the all-potency of Spirit. The formation of the Christ, the Son, in the individual follows the same law and involves the whole man, spirit, soul, and body. The changes that take place in the mind and in the body of one who begins to exercise the faculty of faith should occasion no surprise. Sense states of mind have formed groups of cells and fixed them in consciousness in certain relations that are not in accord with spiritual law. The activity of faith in mind and body breaks up these crystallized cells, builds up new combinations and establishes them in the body in divine order and harmony. Thus the soul (Sarai) that seems barren of fruit is by faith in Spirit made to bring forth joyously (Isaac).

This is a lesson of encouragement to those who are faithful yet see no visible fruits of their faith. Jehovah said, "Fear not, Abram: I am thy shield, *and* thy exceeding great reward." Whoever works under the divine law is protected, and the result is sure to come. Active faith in the spiritual powers of Being is productive of tremendous results: "I will multiply thy seed as the stars of the heavens." The outward evidence of the inward reality may be delayed because we are holding in mind some idea that prevents the manifestation. It is estimated that the best telescopes reveal as many as two billion stars. This illustrates the generative power of faith working in the formless substance of spiritual being. Things of form are limited and can bring but limited reward. Working in the formless, one is working in the free range of the whole expanse of the heavens, and the results are like the innumerable stars, beyond all computation.

The fulfillment of this faith in God may not come at once. A way must be opened in the consciousness for its descent into externality. But keep

on believing. "He believed in Jehovah; and he
reckoned it to him for righteousness." Then find
out why you do not have the visible evidence. Abram
asked for specific evidence. He said, "O Lord Jehovah, whereby shall I know that I shall inherit
it?" Then follows instructions for a sacrifice.
Some ideas on the sense plane must be sacrificed,
especially those which have been holding back the
demonstration. A heifer, a she-goat, a ram, a turtle
dove, and a young pigeon are mentioned. These
stand for ideas of physical strength, human will, and
subconscious resistance. The idea of physical
strength should be given up for the realization that
its source is spiritual. Sacrifice your human will and
the divine will will work its perfect way in you.
Deny away all subconscious resistance to the workings of divine law. Let peace and patience pervade
your mind, while ever knowing that swiftness is
characteristic of all spiritual action. Look for a
swift fulfillment of all that you are holding in faith
and if it is delayed, know that some sacrifices are
necessary. In all this process continue to drive away,
by denial, all the "birds of prey," as Abram did.
Faith is quickened and increased by a denial of all
inability, which seems real to the mind of sense.
Affirm that the boundless, limitless power that creates the stars, can accomplish in your world all that
it has promised or that you have desired.

Abram's greatest desire was to bring forth a son.
Our greatest desire is like unto it, for it is to bring
forth *the* Son, the Christ, in our consciousness and in

our life. God's promise applies in both cases, and the method is the same: the limited ideas of sense must be sacrificed for the limitless power of Spirit.

It was revealed to Abram that he should henceforth be called Abraham, which means "father of a multitude." The change in name always denotes a change in character that is so pronounced that the old name will no longer apply to the new person. We read that Jacob's name was changed to Israel, Simeon became Peter, and Saul's name was changed to Paul. The change of name applies to every one who changes from sense to Spirit, as is indicated in Revelation 2:17: "I will give him [that overcometh sense] a white stone, and upon the stone a new name written, which no one knoweth but he that receiveth it." The new name, Abraham, "father of a multitude," when we apply it individually means that our faith is to be expressed by bringing the multitude of our thoughts into the realm of Spirit and under the guidance of the Christ.

Through Abraham God called His "chosen people." Some have thought that God's choice of a particular nation or race is out of harmony with the idea of fatherly love and impartiality toward all His children, and so have rejected part of God's purpose before they understand it in its wholeness. Justice to all is seen when the "elect" are considered in their rightful place in the divine plan of redemption. The Jews are the seed of Abraham, and through them is the whole human race blessed by the coming of the Christ.

When faith (Abraham) first catches this large vision of its good "as the stars of the heavens" it is not concerned with details, which will work themselves out later. The particular channel through which this great expression would come was not revealed to Abraham in the first promise. The specific thing, the birth of a son to Sarah, to be called Isaac, was a much later revelation. All the facts in connection with the call of Abraham, his experiences, and the several promises made to him by Jehovah God are very important to us, for the great plan of redemption cannot be understood without them. All these promises have not been fulfilled even as yet, but the word of God stands sure, and there can be no failure in their fulfillment.

Critics have accused religion of being too general, abstract, and idealistic. Some have said that the teachings of Jesus are not "practical" in this age. These critics are invariably looking at religion from a general and abstract point of view. They consider such promises as the one made to Abraham that he should be the father of a great nation, with descendants as many as the stars of heaven, rather than the terse and very definite promise "Sarah, thy wife, shall bear thee a son."

Religion was not a speculative philosophy to Lazarus, to the ten lepers, to the man born blind. Some say that Jesus could heal the sick, give sight to the blind and raise the dead because He was the only son of God, therefore an exception and unique among men. Yet we find His disciples performing the same "miracles" after He had ascended. Peter cured the man sick with the palsy and many others. Paul performed many healings and even restored life in at least one instance. For nearly three hundred years the Christians of the early church experienced these healing "miracles" almost daily, confirming the promise of Jesus "He that believeth on me, the works that I do shall he do also; and greater works than these shall he do."

From a careful study of Genesis, especially the story of Abraham, we should be able to see that our religion is either a purely speculative philosophy or a practical principle applicable to daily living, depending upon our point of view and our understanding of it.

Jehovah on His first contact with Abraham made him a certain promise, namely that his descendants should become a great nation in which all the people of the earth would be blessed. This was rather abstract and indefinite: Abraham was to leave his old life and environment, give up his home, and go into a new and unknown land (state of consciousness).

Jehovah made His second appearance to Abraham when he was camped under the oak of Moreh, in the land of Shechem. At that time he was on his way down into Egypt, keeping the commandment "Get thee out of thy country . . . unto the land that I will show thee." Here he received Jehovah's promise "Unto thy seed will I give this land." This shows us that Abraham is progressing in understanding, that God is becoming more definite to him, and the promise more specific.

Jehovah next appeared to Abraham after he had separated himself from Lot and returned to the land of Canaan. This time the promise was still more definite, namely that Jehovah would give him and his seed forever this very land that he saw and walked upon, to the eastward, westward, northward, and southward. Nothing indefinite or theoretical about that! Yet the promise was still indefinite as regards the descendants who were to be as numerous as the dust of the earth. The indefinite nature of this part of the promise was due to Abraham's lack of understanding and complete faith, for somewhere in his mind was a doubting thought caused by the fact that his wife, Sarah, was barren and could have no children. When we doubt God's promises by speculating how He can keep them, or when we set up limitations on His power, we of course fail to comprehend, and the promises seem vague and indefinite.

The next time the promise was repeated is recorded in the 15th chapter of Genesis. Here we are told that Abraham "believed in Jehovah; and he reckoned it to him for righteousness." Also for the first time Abraham was bold enough to ask God for additional details and for a definite understanding as regards the promise. The answer to this prayer was immediate. In a dream God revealed to Abraham that his descendants should be sojourners in a strange land (Egypt) for four hundred years, and

should then come into Canaan with great substance
and power to claim it as their own country.

God's promises are not vague nor veiled in mystery. If they seem so or if anything about our religion seems hazy or indefinite, it is because our understanding has not been developed sufficiently to
comprehend the fullness of it. Through his repeated contacts with God Abraham grew in understanding, as we also shall grow by continually "practicing the presence."

In the 18th chapter of Genesis we have a most
interesting account of another of Jehovah's appearances to Abraham. This time Abraham was sitting
"in the tent door," inactive because of "the heat of
the day." The tent was pitched under the oaks of
Mamre, and Jehovah's appearance here was the most
definite of all. The oak tree denotes something
strong and protective. In many places in the Bible
God's protection is compared to an oak tree. We
are told that God is our strength, our deliverance,
our refuge from the storm. Mamre means "fat-
ness," firmness, vigor, strength, and symbolizes en-
durance, renewed life, and abundant substance.
Thus we see that faith (Abraham) has in and
around itself everything needful for growth and for
its firm establishment in consciousness.

"He lifted up his eyes and looked, and, lo, three
men stood over against him." Faith must "lift up"
its eyes above all material things and look to the
spiritual as the source of all. Having done that, it
will perceive the truth in its triune aspect. Abraham

saw Jehovah as "three men." Jehovah is always the central figure, but we must not lose sight of the fact that, although the one Mind is the omnipresent source of all, it manifests itself as a trinity of spirit, soul, and body, or spirit, consciousness, and substance. When faith lifts up its eyes and catches this vision, then indeed hath Jehovah appeared unto it, and His promises are sure and clear.

The water that Abraham brought to wash the feet of his guest or guests signifies the necessity for purifying the consciousness by the use of denials. The "morsel of bread" for the strengthening of the heart represents substance in its relation to the renewing of one's inner strength and courage; also the necessity of using affirmation (eating bread) for the growth of the soul. Abraham recognized the triune aspect of Jehovah in manifestation, for he talked to the three as though they were one man, whom he addresses as "my lord." This one is I AM.

If by faith in Spirit we receive the higher ideas and entertain them as though they were realities instead of "figments of the imagination," as the faithless term them, we thereby open the way for a new state of consciousness. Many Truth seekers try to visualize God by thinking of the divine master Jesus and surround themselves with pictures of Him to aid the eye of faith.

Jehovah goes into the details of His former promise to Abraham at greater length because faith has now comprehended God in a more particular and practical way. In the former case Jehovah was

understood in an abstract and transcendent way and
His promise was abstract and vast in scope: that
Abraham should be the father of multitudes. Now
faith sees God in His triune manifestation as spirit,
soul, and body, like unto "three men," which is a
definite and practical conception. The promise is
renewed and brought down to a practical basis.
Abraham is to be the father of a nation, because his
wife Sarah is to give birth to a son. This is a definite
promise that cannot be misunderstood by Abraham
or long postponed by Jehovah.

Since the human race is made up of individuals
all patterned after the one divine-idea man, we can
see in the history of these Bible characters the story
of our own spiritual development both as individuals and as a race. Our understanding of the life of
Abraham will not be complete unless we consider it
in both these relations to us.

Abraham did not doubt God's promise but felt
that it was necessary for him to assist in bringing it
into manifestation in his own way, instead of await-
ing God's good time. It never occurred to him that
such a promise could be fulfilled through Sarah,
who was unable to bear children. Sarah too wanted
to help bring the promise into manifestation but
never gave a thought to its being done in the obvious
and natural way, because her mind had set up limitations. Hence Abraham took his wife's maid
Hagar and had a son by her.

The name Hagar means "flight," "wanderer or
fugitive," or "to flee one's country." Metaphysi-

cally, she represents the natural or animal soul in man, which is a servant to the higher spiritual soul, represented by Sarah. The thoughts of the animal soul are not lifted up to a very high plane and are therefore likely to be sensual, selfish, or unholy, which reacts to produce a state of fear or uncertainty (wanderer). This sensual must give way to the spiritual. It cannot stand in the presence of the Christ Truth but flees before it (flight). Hagar's son, being the fruit of the union of faith with natural will and affection on a lower plane of expression, was not recognized by Jehovah as the heir of the promise.

There is an important lesson in this for every one who is growing in faith and seeking to bring forth the fruits of Spirit according to the promise. No true spiritual demonstration is made unless the divine law is recognized and obeyed. When we try to demonstrate Truth through our own personal will and effort, we find that we fall short.

Paul gives us in Galatians 4:21-31 an interpretation of this allegory. He calls Sarah the freewoman and Hagar the bondmaid. We who are born of Spirit in the Christ consciousness are sons of the freewoman and "the children of promise." Those born of the bondmaid (sense) are of the flesh and are cast out from the inheritance of Spirit.

Ishmael means "whom God hears," "whom God understands." Metaphysically, it signifies the fruit of the thoughts of the natural man at work in the flesh. However, God hears and understands the

outer man of flesh as well as the inner man of Spirit,
for he too must be redeemed from error and corruption. The name Ishmael can also be said to signify that state of consciousness which recognizes
God but which, because of the seeming opposition
of the outer world, does not express itself according
to the highest standards. In other words, he represents personality, which has its real source in the
I AM, but which goes wrong in its activity. In its
struggle to attain light or understanding it contacts
the outer world and becomes confused or involved
in error.

The time has now arrived in the development of
spiritual consciousness when faith (Abraham) must
be fully awakened to the truth that all belief in the
expression of sensuality must be entirely put away.
Sodom is to be destroyed. But the man of faith is
not yet entirely out of his sense consciousness.
Sodom means "hidden wiles," representing an obscure or concealed thought habit. Gomorrah means
"material force," or a state of mind adverse to the
law of Spirit. These wicked cities of the plain are
located within man, and before he can come into a
realization of the promised "son" that he so desires,
he must consent to a thorough purification from
these sins. The purification is by fire and must be
absolutely complete.

The remainder of the chapter concerns Jehovah's
revelation to Abraham of His intention utterly to
destroy Sodom and Gomorrah because of their great
wickedness; also Jehovah's agreement to save Sodom

if only ten righteous men could be found in it. The tendency to plead to be allowed to keep old habits of thought on the ground that there is some good in them is a characteristic of man's early stages of development. But error must be wholly wiped out of the consciousness, and the sooner we consent to accept the fullness of the regenerative law, the sooner will we enter the kingdom. Sodom signifies hidden wiles, and we try very hard to save some of our secret habits and sense thoughts. Because we have indulged them all our life and our ancestors have done so before us, we think there must be some good in them. At first we reason that there must be quite a few good things in the old thoughts, ideas, and ways. Then we are a little less sure about there being "fifty" and we come down to "ten." But there are not even ten righteous, and the old consciousness must be destroyed.

Sodom represents the very lowest form of sense desire in the procreative center. Sodomy is to this day the name of an unmentionable sin. Yet the spiritually minded Abraham persisted in the belief that there must be some good in Sodom. Jehovah showed him otherwise. The tendency to plead that there must be good in sense habits persists very strongly. We cannot conceive why these functions, which seem so necessary to the reproduction of the race, should not be under the divine law. This is because we have not yet awakened to the fact that they are but an external and counterfeit expression, a degenerate imitation, of divine reproduction.

Do not hold the thought that your so-called natural functions are divine. They are great mysteries to the human consciousness, to be understood when we have acquired spiritual wisdom. The race has gone through some strange experiences, and wonderful revelations come to those who get beneath the surface of things. There are those walking the earth today who could startle the world with revelations of Truth about the things right under our eyes that we do not see. Resolutely turn your back upon all the forms of sense thought and seek no excuse for them. Then you will gradually begin to see the light within the light.

Mysteries of Genesis

CHAPTER SEVEN

THE FRUITS OF FAITH

Study: Genesis, chapters 21 and 22.

Affirmative Prayer

*My whole being is lifted up and re-
newed when I joyously unify myself
with spiritual life and substance.*

The Fruits of Faith

ISAAC, A SYMBOL OF JOY

IT REQUIRES the whole story of Israel from Abraham to Jesus Christ to picture fully the growth and spiritualization of the whole man. The unfolding and lifting into spiritual consciousness includes the body of man, which must be unified with the soul and spirit into one perfect being capable of manifesting the spiritual substance and character of God ideated in the beginning. In spirit, soul, and body we come into the perfect expression of Godlikeness—one man, one Christ, one God.

Israel, the nation, in its highest significance implies this unity of spirit, soul, and body, the perfect spiritual consciousness. It is an amalgamation of Egypt, the seemingly material, with Assyria, the psychic forces, and the original Abraham stock, which means faith in God.

Faith is the foundation faculty or power of mind through which spiritual man is brought forth. Christ was the consummation of the aspirations of Abraham. Israel claims Abraham as its father through Isaac, the son after his own heart, who had a thirst for the things of Spirit. Even in his youth Isaac was willing to have his body offered up as a sacrifice, thus symbolizing "the Lamb of God." He thus represents the true divine sonship. His name means "laughter," which signifies the joy of the new birth. Man rejoices greatly in his privilege of expressing the Son of God. Spiritual consciousness of oneness with God the Father should bring the greatest joy possible to any person.

Isaac was born after Abraham and Sarah were both past the age of bringing forth. So we, when born of the Spirit through faith, are born not "of the will of the flesh, nor of the will of man, but of God." The natural man has no power to bring forth "the new man" in Christ Jesus. The natural man brings forth Hagar's son, who is not the chosen heir. The new man is a "new creature," begotten not by flesh but by the divine word. This refers to the forming of a new state of consciousness, fulfilling the hope that Paul expressed to the Galatians: that "Christ be formed in you."

This forming of the Christ in the individual involves the whole man, spirit, soul, and body. The fall into the Adam consciousness has tended to disintegrate this perfect trinity, but in the Christ consciousness the three are unified and harmonized under the divine law of Being in its true expression. A new man in every sense of the word is actually formed through a divine begetting, quickening, and growth. If this causes changes in the mind and the body they should occasion no surprise. Certain states of mind have formed cells and fixed them in relationships that are not in accord with divine perfection. These crystallized cells are broken up by the activity of the Christ mind, new ones are built and all are established in relationships of divine order and harmony.

Sometimes when the first stirrings of the new life within are felt by one who does not understand that the renewing of the mind necessarily transforms the body, a fear arises. Old race ideas of disease come into mind. Various systems of healing may be tried to stop the regenerating work that is going on in the consciousness. It can be readily seen that such interference with the working of Spirit is not right, nor is it safe. Those who are in any stage of the new birth should consecrate themselves wholly to God and should trust Him absolutely with their bodies. They should realize that no doctor or any man in sense consciousness understands the workings of Spirit and should keep hands off. "It is not yet made manifest what we shall be." Not even the most enlightened of the Spirit yet know the glories of the redeemed body. They must trust day by day while the transformation from natural to spiritual is going on and keep their eyes fixed upon their divine perfection as it is standardized in Jesus Christ.

When Isaac was weaned, Ishmael, Hagar's son, mocked him. This is the experience of every one in the new birth. The thoughts that are the fruits of the mind of the flesh rise up within him and mock the new man. Here the overcomer has a definite work to do. Hagar the bondmaid (animal soul) and

her son (fleshly desires) must be cast out. Abraham
was grieved when Hagar was banished. We sometimes grieve over giving up the fruits of material
thinking brought forth by the natural man.

In the development of the spiritual faculties, of
which faith (Abraham) is one, there is a movement
of the consciousness in an ascending scale, which is
felt and understood by the one having the experience but difficult to explain to those who have not
yet entered that phase of development. The faculty
of faith grows stronger at each trial, and when it is
obedient to the Lord as its divine guide, it finds an
added pleasure in the exercise of the functions of
both the mind and the body at every upward step.
Every function of man's organism is spiritual at
its foundation, and when exercised as intended by
Divine Mind every breath and every heartbeat is a
song of joy. Even the most earthly functions may
be spiritualized and become sources of unending
pleasure, but when these earthly functions are under
the control of the animal mind of man, they become
demoralizers of the body. Under divine guidance this
demoralization produced by mere animalism may be
harmonized and purified through the descent of the
fires of Spirit. This is what happened to Sodom and
Gomorrah, which represent the functions pertaining
to generation.

When we have faith in God and the ways of
Spirit, we are willing to give up all our material
pleasures if such be the instruction of the inner
guide. This is symbolized by the sacrifices so often

referred to in the history of the Children of Israel. The body and its vital forces are in perpetual action, which is progressive under the divine law. When that law is disregarded there is retrogression that brings a sense of discomfort and finally of pain. It is frequently through pain that we are brought to see that we have departed from the law of our being. Then we should hasten to find the law of being that will give us real pleasure without the inharmony.

This is illustrated in the experience of Abraham. After giving up mere animal gratification (Hagar) and purifying the mind of sense thoughts (banishing Hagar and Ishmael), a greater pleasure was experienced from a more interior or spiritual action of the same function. Isaac was the fulfillment of Abraham's greatest desire. But this use of the bodily functions must also be raised to a higher plane of consciousness. On each of the ascending stages in bodily transmutation there is a residuum of the last preceding stage remaining in consciousness. This too must be purified in order that the whole man may be a fit temple for the Holy Spirit.

The story of the near sacrifice of Isaac also illustrates the same truth, that the pleasures of sense must be given up in order that we may have the consciousness of the greater satisfactions of Spirit. Like Abraham we must be willing to give up the pleasures of sense without question. Being willing and obedient in submitting our sensations to the law of Spirit, we then find that we do not sacrifice at all the real inner joy but only its coarser expression in physical generation, which is represented by the ram.

It seemed that this experience of Abraham's demanded the slaying of Isaac, the whole consciousness of joy. In these degrees of unfoldment there are trials as well as triumphs, and those who have but a transient faith in the wisdom and power of Spirit are apt to give up and turn back before the process is complete. The "land of Moriah" where Abraham was sent to make his sacrifice means the "bitterness of Jehovah." So we find sometimes that in the changes that take place in consciousness there are bitter experiences, and it takes a strong faith to believe that good will come out of them. Yet it always does when there is a steadfast obedience to God and faith in His goodness. The successful overcoming of such trials gives great power to the body and brings a great reward. Abraham became the father of a multitude as numerous "as the stars of the heavens, and as the sand which is upon the seashore."

The child was not sacrificed although Abraham took every step in preparation. After this test, successfully passed, the angel of the Lord repeated the promise of the covenant "By myself have I sworn, saith Jehovah . . . and in thy seed shall all the nations of the earth be blessed; because thou hast obeyed my voice."

In the regeneration man must be willing to sacrifice his greatest pleasure in life (Isaac). But when he has given up willingly, made the spiritual surrender, he finds that it is not his joy of life that he sacrifices but only the sensuous aspect of joy.

Faith in God (Abraham) and obedience to the divine law brings forth a serene peace and joy. Christians well know that the development of faith and obedience does cause one to become inwardly happy and outwardly serene. Jesus had this inward happiness, and He tried to pass it on to His disciples: "These things have I spoken unto you, that my joy may be in you, and *that* your joy may be made full."

As one feels a certain inner satisfaction after having done a great deed, so after having repeatedly followed the promptings of Spirit there is an accumulated fund of satisfaction that finally breaks forth in laughter. Isaac was not born until Abraham and Sarah had come to old age—had accumulated a "faith consciousness." We notice the different kinds of laughter in this allegory. Abraham laughed questioningly, hopefully when it was announced that Sarah would bear a son. Sarah laughed incredulously but with a wistful joy when the promise was announced to her. Both laughed joyfully and with thanksgiving and all Sarah's friends laughed with her when Isaac was born.

Religion is not the dolorous thing that many have pictured it, much to its loss and to ours as well. On the contrary it should make man joyful. God is not to be served as a taskmaster but in the spirit of happiness. In Deuteronomy we read, "Because thou servedst not Jehovah thy God with joyfulness, and with gladness of heart, by reason of the abundance

of all things; therefore shalt thou serve thine enemies . . . in hunger, and in thirst, and in nakedness, and in want of all things." If one's prayers
are not answered or one fails to demonstrate, here
perhaps is where the reason may be found.

It is found by those who persistently exercise
faith in God that there is generated in the mind a
condition that gradually grows into a conviction of
the permanent presence of divine substance within,
and this gives rise to the most exquisite joy. This
inward ecstasy is what gives the countenance of peace
to the saint and of illuminated purity to the sister
of mercy. It is experienced by all who pass into the
second degree of faith (Isaac, son of Abraham).

Joy and happiness open channels that are closed
by habitual woe and melancholy, channels through
which numberless blessings come to one. A leading
characteristic of joyous people is the way in which
prosperity is manifested for them. "Isaac sowed in
that land, and found in the same year a hundredfold
. . . And Jehovah blessed him. . . . and he had
possessions of flocks, and possessions of herds, and a
great household." There is a perpetual flow of pure
life essence coming through the inner centers of consciousness, which is the joy of Christ in us seeking
expression.

Isaac was not noted as a man of achievement.
He represents the serenity, peace, and joy that man
has when he accepts spiritual things as real and lives
"as seeing him who is invisible."

The happy Isaac consciousness claimed its counterpart in Rebekah, whose name signifies "a noose" or "captivating snare," meaning a young woman whose great beauty ensnares men. Faith and obedience (Abraham) brings forth joy, and joy (Isaac) links itself with the beauty of nature without. "And Isaac went out to meditate in the field at eventide: and he lifted up his eyes, and saw . . . And Rebekah lifted up her eyes . . . and he loved her." Thus is portrayed the union of the devout, joyous nature with the soul of love.

The Isaac faculty in man has a double mission. Isaac was the connecting link between Abraham and Israel; that is, between faith in God and rulership or manifestation of God. He also reopens the hidden springs of life (wells) and keeps the soul consciously connected with its inner source. Isaac was not a well digger so much as a well "reopener." Abraham had dug the wells. Faith delves into the deep things of Spirit and unearths the pure life essence. In the beginning of spiritual unfoldment, however, the outer senses (Philistines) stultify this fine substance and life of Spirit. The Philistines represent unregenerate material thoughts that "fill the earth," the channels of spiritual expression.

Isaac's first well was named Esek, which signifies violence or contention. A warring takes place in the valley (subconsciousness) between the animal desires (the Philistine herdsmen) and the awakening spiritual thoughts. The new energy and vigor of life that man gains by his conscious contact with Spirit is claimed at once by the sense desires to be used for their gratification and pleasure. They would take this fine essence and energy to build up sense rather than to build up the spiritual nature. Thus contention and strife arise.

The second well was called Sitnah, which also signifies strife and hatred. The material sense thoughts (Philistines) do not give up easily but follow the individual a long way on his path to development of spiritual consciousness. However we read that Isaac's third well, called Rehoboth, signifying a broad place or enlargement, was not taken by the Philistines. Material thoughts cannot continue to follow and to annoy the man who is persistent in his determination to find the "water of life."

At this stage of the individual's development comes Abimelech, king of the Philistines, whose name signifies the unregenerate will of the sense man. With him he brings Ahuzzath (selfishness) and Phicol (speech or arguments) and tries to make an agreement with Isaac. The will (Abimelech) believes that it is the rightful ruler of man and that all the rich substance that comes to man from Spirit is for the gratification of sense desires. Having witnessed the ever-increasing power and possessions of Isaac, who represents divine sonship, Abimelech (the will) fears the loss of his own rule and possessions.

The divine son, Christ, does not destroy but fulfills and saves. Error eventually brings on its own destruction, but the error seems to flourish along with the good during a certain period of development—the wheat and the tares are allowed to grow together until the harvest. The harvest time came when the Israelites, under Joshua, took possession of the Promised Land. Even then the Philistines made several successful comebacks and had to be defeated again and again.

There were seven wells altogether, culminating in the one named Beer-sheba, "well of the oath," or "seventh well." This symbolizes the establishment of a right relation in consciousness between the seven creative centers in natural man and the spiritual powers of the Christ man. "And he builded an altar there, and called upon the name of Jehovah." The whole allegory explains the struggle for possession of the life generated in man's body. This contention takes place between the higher and the lower natures of the individual—the spiritual soul and the animal soul—at a certain period in spiritual development. Beer-sheba is the place where the altar of victory is set up and God is given the thanks.

Mysteries of Genesis

CHAPTER EIGHT

THE MENTAL SUPPLANTS THE PHYSICAL

Study: Genesis, chapters 27 and 28.

Affirmative Prayer

I now assert and maintain the dominion that God has given me, and I am master over all my thoughts, words, and actions.

The Mental Supplants the Physical

JACOB AND ESAU

THE DEVELOPMENT of man goes steadily forward. New phases of character are constantly being added to his consciousness and the old ones toned down or eliminated. Isaac, the inner joyous life current, gradually builds up a physical body of great vitality and at the same time develops an active mentality. These two phases of life are represented by Isaac's twin sons Jacob and Esau. They were twins, but Esau was slightly the older, which fact under the Hebrew law gave him the rights of the eldest son and made him Isaac's heir. Metaphysically this denotes that physical vigor comes first in this phase of development, but the mind accompanies it as a close second. Jacob had hold of Esau's heel as they were born, showing that the mental phase is directly connected with the physical and holds it in check at all times, even from the beginning.

The difference between Esau and Jacob is given us in Jacob's own words in Gen. 27:11: "Behold, Esau my brother is a hairy man, and I am a smooth man." The Arabic word for "hairy," the best translators tell us, has a connotation of intemperance or licentiousness. In the Epistle to the Hebrews Paul calls Esau a "fornicator." This may be taken in a literal sense or in the sense of one who commits spiritual adultery, that is, who is unfaithful to God, divine love. The name "Esau" also signifies "one swept away," or "one who rushes forward wildly and impulsively." He is the very antipode of Jacob, "the smooth," clean, and reliable man. The word "smooth" is used in the story of David's victory over Goliath; he took "five smooth stones out of the brook." Jesus said, "The prince of the world cometh: and he hath nothing in me"; that is, he cannot find a footing or place by which to catch hold.

It would be wrong to think that Esau had no chance to develop himself in his higher capacities. He was Jacob's twin, both were brought up in the same godly family, both were sons of joy (Isaac). Where Esau failed was in learning the lesson of self-control. To satisfy an immediate appetite or impulse he would tread "under foot the Son of God."

Esau is unfortunately no uncommon type. As for "smooth" men, very few are smooth to start with. It is the constant rubbing, cutting, and re-shaping that makes them at last "the polished corners of the temple," good and beautiful after the pattern of heaven.

The denunciations of Esau by the prophets Jeremiah, Obadiah, and Malachi were not directed against a man of that name but against a course of conduct such as his. Owing to this it might well appear to Malachi that God loved Jacob and hated

Esau, interpreting the names metaphorically, Jacob
symbolizing the mental man and Esau the physical
or animal man.

Isaac loved Esau better than he loved Jacob. We
must remember that Isaac represents joy in the individual's consciousness, and we can understand how
the physical man seems to supply the needs of joy
more than does the mental. Esau continually
brought venison to please his father.

Rebekah loved Jacob better than she loved Esau.
She symbolizes the beautiful and aesthetic side of
man's nature, the divine natural. As in keeping
with the mother principle in which these twin states
of mind gestated and grew she desires that the mental take precedence over the animal, so she suggests
by her inner imagery that Isaac, the dominant consciousness, place his blessing upon Jacob. This
seems a trick upon a blind old father but is rather
an Oriental illustration of how we are moved by
emotional states of consciousness and how, in our
half-blind understanding, we accept their suggestions. The fact is that the soul (woman, Rebekah)
is constantly making suggestions to us in dreams,
visions, and intuitive flashes. These suggestions
may sometimes be for our highest good and sometimes they may not. Spiritual understanding must
determine this point and decide whether we should
follow them or not. Rebekah represents the love
of the ideal, and it is only through Jacob, the mental,
that her ideals can be realized.

Esau's birthright is the body and the all-round

development to which it is entitled. It is an inheritance of potential mental powers, which rightly
used will lift the physical man out of the fleshly consciousness to the higher consciousness of the allness
of Divine Mind. Under the natural law of evolution the physical man (Esau) is brought forth first
and has precedence over the intellectual man
(Jacob). However in this allegory the physical man
is overwhelmed by his desire for creature comforts
("pottage") and does not sufficiently value the mind
power that has been given to man. The mental
man, being on a higher plane, naturally draws to
himself the finer forces of being. In consequence
Jacob (the intellect) acquires precedence over Esau
(body consciousness).

The ambitious ideas of the intellect forge far
ahead of the growth of the body. Instead of supplying the body with its natural substance, which is
spiritual, it gives the body consciousness intellectual
ideas (boiled pottage). This results in a temporary
separation in consciousness between the mind and
the body. Esau went his way, and Jacob became a
man rich in the world's goods. Under divine law
however they were twins and the separation was
only apparent. They were to become united again
and share all the blessings that Jacob (intellect) had
gained.

We must remember that the "birthright" that
Esau so willingly bartered away for a mess of "pottage" meant not only a right to the material goods
of his father Isaac but to the spiritual blessings of

the covenant of Abraham, which descending on him,
should through him bless the world. Instead of
"Abraham, Isaac, and Esau," the immortal words
would be "Abraham, Isaac, and Jacob." To a "pro-
fane person" (Heb. 12:16) this would have no
meaning, for spiritual blessings are visionary and
unreal to him.

The name Jacob means "supplanter." In the
development of the spiritual consciousness the supplanting quality finds its true office in replacing selfishness with unselfishness. We who seek to bring
the ideal into active expression in our life know that
to do this we must put into the place occupied by
willful self-seeking an unwavering faith in the unseen God. The sensual must be supplanted by the
spiritual, the apparent by the ideal. The fact that
Jesus approvingly cited the Jewish traditions in His
words "Many shall come from the east and the west,
and shall sit down with Abraham, and Isaac, and
Jacob, in the kingdom of heaven" proves the value
of this supplanting power or power that man has to
change his mind and so remake his consciousness and
his life. It is by the work of conscious re-creation
of his life after the pattern of the divine ideal that
man gains self-dominion and becomes a citizen of
the kingdom of heaven, the inner kingdom of peace
and power.

The mind feels that its claim to the control of
life should come before the claims of physical sense.
By its superior quickness, aided by the soul's (Rebekah's) love of mental acumen, the mental tricks

the physical and secures the blessing of substance and the acknowledged authority in the organism. Then the head rules the heart in us until the touch of Spirit (Jacob's wrestling with the angel) arouses the soul to action and there is another supplanting, this time of the intellect's sterile claims, which are taken over by the soul. In reality the physical body has an equal right with the intellect to the uplifting and refining influence of Spirit. Being twins, they should be treated as equals, the law of the first-born should not be allowed to operate, but both should be blessed and established in the substance of all good things.

When cheated of its due, the body rebels, as Esau did, and the outraged cells react in a disorderly way on the mind. Insane asylums bear witness to the fact that a neglected body will destroy the channels through which the mind is meant to function perfectly in man. The threat of Esau against the life of Jacob represents the inward rebellion that we feel when we change our modes of thought.

To avoid an open conflict the soul (Rebekah) suggests that Jacob flee to her brother Laban at Haran. Laban means "white," "shining," and Haran, "exalted," "mountaineer." This clearly indicates that the attention shall be located in exalted states of mind and united with spiritual intelligence and nonresistance.

When we understand that Jacob, Esau, and all the other persons and places mentioned in these allegories, represent ideas in the mind of a single individual—of you who read about them—then the incidents are more easily reconciled with justice and righteousness.   Jacob, the ambition for higher things, supplants Esau, the contented creature of sense, appropriates his birthright, and receives his blessing.   These are legitimate steps in the upward way of the aspiring soul.   The strong man of sense must be bound and his goods taken away from him, taught Jesus.   If we do not overcome the animal in us it will become our master.   It is easy for a soul to fall under the delusions of sense and go down instead of up.   The law ordained is "that ye go forward."

Before we can deal justly and truly with physical man, we must have the very inspiration of God: no less.   The problem is not a simple one and cannot be solved entirely by intellectual means. When we turn our thought toward the higher realm of invisible Spirit, our vision clears and we perceive that the body is indeed the "temple of God."

All religious observances are symbols of mental processes necessary to the growth of the soul.   One who practices any rite may not at the time understand its significance, but it will be impressed upon his mind and eventually be spiritually understood. Eating bread and drinking wine as representative of the body and the blood of the Lord is practiced as a vital part of the Christian ritual, but how many have the consciousness of the invisible substance and life that the symbols represent?   Baptism also represents the cleansing of the mind of impure thoughts, and it should be followed by a daily washing away by denial of every thought arising in the mind that in any way partakes of falsity. Circumcision is a reminder that the lusts of sensuality are to be cut off by those who seek the higher or heavenly estate.

Whether or not this rite was necessary to a Christian was discussed by the early church leaders, as set forth in the 15th chapter of Acts. They decided that cleansing of the heart was the great and only way of salvation. Paul taught that we are saved by grace and not by any outward ceremony.

However, we who are seeking the spiritual meaning of all things should not cast aside as nonsensical a rite so widely practiced and by so many people. Circumcision represents the elimination of sensuality, a matter of vital importance to humanity. The human family on this earth is dominated by sensual thoughts and practices that from a spiritual standpoint approach insanity. The whole race has fallen into a lust for sensation (Satan) that drains the body of the very elixir of life and leaves it a stranded wreck "sans teeth, sans eyes, sans taste, sans everything."

Man has directive power over all the faculties of the mind and the functions of the body, and his work as a developing soul is to build a man in which all of these work in harmony. To do this man must see to it that no one faculty or function is allowed to develop beyond the others and thus rob them of the body substance and life that they require to remain active. But that is just what sensation has done in the human family on this earth.

Sex sensation, represented by Judas among the disciples of Jesus, has under the impulse of sensation (Satan) developed a dominating personality that makes slaves of all the other faculties, steals their substance, and finally wrecks the body. Judas is represented as carrying the food for the other disciples. He was a thief and finally betrayed his Master into the hands of His enemies (disintegrating forces) through whom the life was driven out of His body.

This is one of the most delicate subjects in the discussion of sin and its effects upon the body. Men are so dominated by sex habits that they will not listen to even the mention of a remedy for their ills when sex mastery is advocated. Nearly all Christian metaphysicians have discovered the same thing, but they also know that the error has become so entrenched in the race mind that it is unwise to recommend an immediate arbitrary stoppage of the habit. The one and only way to gain the mastery under the divine law, as advised by the apostle, is to "do all to the glory of God." Take it all to God in prayer and you will lift up the serpent of sense, "as Moses lifted up the serpent in the wilderness."

Mysteries of Genesis

CHAPTER NINE

THE SPIRITUAL GAINS PRECE-
DENCE OF THE MENTAL

Study: Genesis, chapters 32 and 33.

Affirmative Prayer

God hath dealt graciously with me, and
I have enough.

The Spiritual Gains Precedence
Of the Mental

JACOB BECOMES ISRAEL

MAN DEVELOPS his faculties in an orderly manner when he looks to Divine Mind as the one and only guide. But he does not always seek this inner wisdom, and the result is a disorderly development. Jacob represents the mind in man that directs the physical body (Esau) in all its acts. In divine order Jacob should be born first—we should think before we act —but we find that as a rule people do not reflect and then act, and especially is this true among people who are in the first stages of their race journey.

The natural man in his immature consciousness is moved by desire and not by rational thinking. He seeks to satisfy appetite regardless of higher law and sells his birthright for a mess of pottage. When understanding (Jacob) takes the ascendancy, there is an entire change. Jacob went toward Haran ("enlightened," "mountainous"). The significance of this sentence is that when we let our meditations and blessings fall upon the "knowing" part of ourselves (Jacob instead of Esau) we go into a higher mental state or an exalted condition of mind, wherein we receive a higher and clearer conception of things spiritual.

On his journey to Haran, which had a double purpose—to escape the wrath of the disappointed Esau and "to take him a wife"—Jacob came to a certain place where he tarried all night because "the sun was set." He took one of the stones that abounded in the place for a pillow and lay down to sleep. This incident signifies that when we are going through an emotional experience that is leading us upward to a higher spiritual consciousness, we may not understand it, may not have light on it ("the sun was set"); but if like Jacob we tarry there in this darkness in meditation, the messengers of God —ideas of truth—will come to us in the subconsciousness (dream).

Jacob's act of placing a stone under his head signifies the understanding putting itself in a position to unravel the meaning of matter and material conditions. Right there in the very midst of seeming materiality and darkened understanding the visions of the night reveal the ladder that leads from earth to heaven, and the angels of God (spiritual thoughts) ascending and descending upon it. The ladder represents the step-by-step realization by means of which man assimilates the divine ideas of Truth that come to him from Jehovah. Jehovah promised the land to Jacob and his seed and assured Jacob of His continued presence and power: "Behold, I am with thee, and will keep thee whitherso-

ever thou goest, and will bring thee again into this
land; for I will not leave thee . . . And Jacob
awaked out of his sleep, and he said, Surely Jehovah
is in this place; and I knew it not."

God is right here in our midst. Understanding,
when turned toward the omnipresent light of Spirit,
opens its eyes to the astonishing fact that the seemingly material bodies and temporal surroundings con-
ceal the immanent God. Jacob said, "How dreadful is this place! this is none other than the house of
God, and this is the gate of heaven." When divine
wisdom reveals to us that our seemingly physical
body is "none other than the house of God," we are
at first afraid. It seems "dreadful" that we have
made the Father's house "a den of robbers."

In the morning of this new understanding even
the temporal surroundings become holy in our sight.
Like Jacob we set up the common things, the stones
upon which we have slept in ignorance, and pour
the oil of joy and gladness upon them. Then we
name the place (our body temple and its affairs)
Bethel, the "house of God." Jacob took the stone
that he had used for a pillow and made a pillar of
it. Instead of whining over the hardness of his
experience he blessed it and made it a sustaining
point in his mind.

Jacob was awestruck by the tremendous thought
of omnipresence: what seems so commonplace may
be the very house of God, and thinking some true
thought or doing some loving act may be the gate
of heaven. Jacob's vow to be more faithful to God

and to give Him one tenth of all he received is a recognition of God as the source of all that man requires and also of the need of a constant reminder of this fact; hence the agreement to give back the tithe. Those who practice tithing testify that it leads them into an understanding of the relation that God bears to material affairs that they can get in no other way. When a person feels that he has God for a partner in all his financial affairs, he is never afraid of failure or lack.

In his inner consciousness man can make an agreement of this kind with the mind of Spirit and can keep it in his everyday affairs. Many metaphysicians write out and sign agreements of this kind and put them away with the full assurance that they will be carried out by both contracting parties, God and man. It is found by nearly every one who tries this plan that the agreement is fulfilled. If you would have your material affairs prosper, agree with Jehovah to give one tenth of your income to some work dedicated to God. If you keep your part of the agreement, you may rest assured that the Lord will keep His and abundantly prosper you, that your financial affairs will be taken care of without worry or strain on your part, and that you will come into a land where peace and plenty go hand in hand.

When there is recognition, in fact, by the mental (Jacob) of the true nature of the body's essence and of the spiritual nature of all life, we begin the ascent from self to selflessness. We are then willing to give of our thought substance to God, and the house

of God (the body) bears witness to the sincerity of
our vow.

The natural self seeks to hold on to all that it
can gain by fair or unfair means but the heart self,
as soon as it has had a vision of the infinite, seeks in
its turn to give. In this dream Jacob heard the voice
of God saying, "To thee will I give . . ." When
he awoke and came to himself, his quickened heart
echoed in thankful responsiveness, "I will surely
give . . . unto thee."

From Bethel Jacob proceeded on his journey to
Laban to find a wife. Taking a wife represents a
unification of the I AM with the affections. Jacob
was admonished to go to Paddan-aram ("table-
land") to the house of Bethuel ("unity with God"),
and to take a wife from among the daughters of
Laban ("shining," "pure"). This points the way to
a unification with the love principle in its higher
aspects. Jacob had exalted ideas, divine aspirations,
and now it was necessary that love should become
one of his attributes. High ideals, spiritual aspirations, and pure motives are necessary to the union
with the soul that the I AM was about to make.

When love touches the heart, self drops out of
the mind. "Jacob served seven years for Rachel;
and they seemed unto him but a few days, for the
love he had to her." Love in the heart lifts us out
of the time limits of sense consciousness into the joy
of the eternal present. When we forget ourselves
in the service of love, the selflessness of God takes
possession of our being. Yet such is the paradox of

spiritual law: the selfless man is ever the self-possessed man. The higher self in man loves the soul (Rachel) and works joyously to possess it. The higher self also loves the body with an objective, selfless love, and feeds it with the enduring substance of true thought. Jacob was true to Leah. We can sustain the body in health and unfailing strength by recognizing it as the essence of invisible substance to which our mind and soul have given form.

Until love has done its perfect work, man is fearful. Jacob feared to meet Esau. We find it hard to face the full claims of the body after we have cheated it of its birthright, unity with us in spiritual thought. Divine courage must supplant this fear before we are equal to facing the consequences of our self-centered thoughts and to taking up the task of harmonizing all our forces. But the vital power of Spirit animates the body, and it responds readily to our true thought when we give it of our substance. Later Jacob again entered the land of Canaan, as the Lord had promised he should, and then he came in peace to Shechem, where he encamped. His fears gone, he was free to pitch his tent wherever he pleased. So we, studying his example, may overcome the self through the transforming power of love. We may have a vision of the power of God indwelling, and in the patience that this vision teaches us we may cease striving with the personal self and strive only for the possession of the eternal ideal. Thus we make a new name for ourselves, supplanting the former natural self with the divine self. We find our new name written on the white stone that no one else knows, for it is "I."

When love has performed its work in his consciousness, man ceases to struggle against the seeming evils in the world without and turns his attention to overcoming the inharmonies of the world within himself. "Ye have heard that it was said, An eye for an eye, and a tooth for a tooth: but I say unto you, Resist not him that is evil . . . Ye have heard that it was said, Thou shalt love thy neighbor, and hate thine enemy: but I say unto you, Love your enemies, and pray for them that persecute you."

All through the Bible life is compared to a battle but not war: "the battle is Jehovah's." The Lord does not fight ignorance and evil; the foundation of all existence being good, the law is constantly at work reducing error to its exact stature. As man develops in consciousness, both the soul and the body constantly become more refined under the law of Spirit. This causes a seeming struggle sometimes with adverse conditions, materiality, ignorance, and evil.

In this ongoing the higher principles forge ahead, establish states of consciousness, and gather possessions of substance that must afterward be distributed to the lower principles. Jacob represents the soul that has become rich on an advanced plane of consciousness. A time comes when an evening-up process begins and the body (Esau) must be given some of the riches of the soul. The soul does not like to enter into struggles to overcome material habits, but it is necessary that it do so. The name of the ford Jabbok means "wrestling," and the inference is that it was hard for Jacob to put aside the things that he loved and to enter alone into the invisible to wrestle with the forces of the subconscious or sense consciousness in darkness. This struggle with the physical is illustrated in the overcoming by Jesus in the garden of Gethsemane. The error is pressed out and the rich oil of reality saved.

The life in the subconsciousness has several planes of action. In the deep recesses of the nerves it sends its energy to and fro, coming to the surface here and there in flesh and blood sensation. There is a strong man down there whom the average person knows little about. He lives so far below the plane of common consciousness, that the great majority go through their whole life without making his acquaintance. This man is pure nature, the foundation of the body. Without him we could not take a form, and it is his tenacity that keeps our organism intact. He belongs to nature and is universal; hence when the individual attempts to control him and to lift him up, there is resistance, and a severe struggle with him is inevitable. "The flesh lusteth against the Spirit, and the Spirit against the flesh."

The mind controls the body through the nerves. There is a great nerve leader, the sciatic nerve, running down the leg through the hollow of the thigh, and the will acts directly through this nerve. When

the individual (Jacob) exercises his I AM power in
the effort to control the natural man and to make a
unity between Spirit above and the divine natural
within, there follows a letting go of human will—
Jacob's thigh is out of joint. A great light of understanding breaks in upon the struggling soul when
it discovers that there is a divine-natural body, and
it clings to that inner life and strength until it brings
to the surface the blessing of perpetual physical vigor.
Jacob said, "I will not let thee go, except thou
bless me."

The blessing carried with it a new name, Israel;
that is, one who has striven with God and with men,
and has prevailed. Israel is one who is a prince and
has power as regards both God and man, the spiritual and the material.

After this experience we can appreciate why
Jacob was willing to make amends to Esau (the
body), whom he had cheated and neglected all these
years. When the soul has for a time been lifted
above the body and has ignored its natural needs
there is a subconscious feeling of injustice and a
fear of the results. An awareness of having disregarded divine law makes man afraid without being
able to recall the cause of his fear. People who let
the ambitious intellect (Jacob) override the demands
and rights of the body (Esau) eventually find themselves afraid and anxious to make restitution to the
body. Jacob had passed through this struggle and
arrived at the realization of his unity with the twin
brother. He was now ready to share his wealth:

the intellect would pour out upon the body consciousness some of the substance that it had accumulated.

One can change one's attitude toward the body and thus change the body itself by following the advice of Paul: "Be ye transformed by the renewing of your mind." Do not judge by the appearance, do not call your body temple evil, or corruptible flesh; do not fall into the error of mortal mind. See in the body what Jacob saw, the face of God; for it is ever the temple of the living God.

Jacob, now become Israel, was reunited with Esau after he crossed the ford Jabbok (wrestling). The universal law of the unity of all things was fulfilled. The way in which the mind (Israel) projects its thoughts toward the body (Esau) is symbolized in the way in which Rachel and her children, Leah and her children, and the handmaids with their children, were presented to Esau. The handmaids were presented first because they represent physical thoughts. Leah and her children, presented next, represent intellectual thoughts. Rachel (most beloved) and her son Joseph were presented last and represent the spiritual thoughts. Then Israel himself "passed over before them, and bowed himself to the ground seven times, until he came near to his brother," which means that the I AM in its sevenfold nature humbles itself in the presence of materiality until it has established the unity or kinship "brother" in the consciousness.

The body always obeys the conscious or subconscious behests of the mind. "Esau ran to meet him, and embraced him, and fell on his neck, and kissed him: and they wept." He refused at first to accept the proffered gifts of Israel. The body at first feels its own completeness and resists the rich ideas that the mind has developed in its unfoldment. Jacob (the mind) said, "Receive my present at my hand; forasmuch as I have seen thy face, as one seeth the face of God."

Job says, "Yet in my flesh shall I see God." Jesus said, "He that hath seen me hath seen the Father." The mind must ideate the body as God substance. This will raise the body to the higher consciousness of its innate divinity. The I AM does not make spiritual union with the body until it sees it as the pure and holy temple of God.

Mysteries of Genesis

CHAPTER TEN

MAN DEVELOPS SPIRITUAL FACULTIES

Study: Genesis, chapters 29 and 30.

Affirmative Prayer

"I press on toward the goal unto the prize of the high calling of God in Christ Jesus."

Man Develops Spiritual Faculties

THE TWELVE SONS OF JACOB

AN ALLEGORY is a description of one thing under the image of another. It suggests but does not specifically state a meaning. A key to its interpretation is necessary, and this is usually given in the proper names that are used. By the employment of such symbols the Bible describes man in his wholeness, spirit, soul, and body. The names of men, places, tents, temples in every case have a meaning relative to the character of man. Mental states are thus described, and it is important that the individual who seeks spiritual wisdom for his regeneration shall be able to understand the allegory by use of the key hidden in the names.

An example of this is the name Jacob, which means "supplanter," one who gradually supplants and takes the place of the natural man in the consciousness of the individual and of the race. To accomplish this great work it is necessary that the individualized I AM shall have certain experiences and develop certain faculties essential to the higher-type man that is to follow.

Mystics tell us that man passes through twelve

stages in his spiritual development. Each of these is a particular state of consciousness developed by a presiding ego or faculty. The last and highest state of consciousness is that complete, twelve-sided spiritual character attained by Jesus the Christ. This final attainment of the twelvefold man reveals the spiritual man, the image and likeness created in the beginning. These states may all be active in the individual consciousness at the same time, but the dominant one will indicate the point the person has reached in his development.

Jacob was overdeveloped intellectually and robbed his body (Esau) of its rightful heritage of life. This wrong was atoned for when he divided his accumulated wealth with Esau. In the meantime he had developed the spiritual side of his life and had brought forth a number of faculties (sons).

The approach to the study of soul and spirit is necessarily through man's mind. The philosophers, ancient and modern, are a powerful influence in molding thought. By analysis, correlation, and synthesis man's thought power is developed and the abstract becomes unified with the concrete. Sir James Jeans, the eminent British scientist, says it may be that the Gods that determine our fate are our own minds, working on our brain cells and, through them, on the world without.

Some degree of at-one-ment between mind and its organ, the brain, is required to bring about the fulfillment of our ideals. The brain must become sensitive in two directions, to the world of Spirit within as well as to the world of things without. It stands as a doorway that has been open only to the stimuli from without but must now open our thoughts to the world within as well.

To this end the brain, or rather the whole nervous system—for it is all one and all "brain"—has developed certain specialized functions in the work of evolving mind and body. There are twelve of these specialized functions, each with its center in a definite ganglion in the physical organism.

These ganglia are themselves capable of being developed until they function with an efficiency ever approaching perfection. Such perfection is the aim of our Hindu and other friends who practice certain methods of breathing, dieting, and fasting. These methods have much to recommend them, but they sometimes have results undesirable or even dangerous when practiced by those who do not have the necessary understanding of spiritual law.

The faculties can also be developed by mental methods. Concentration of thought upon one of the centers will set up a vibration that causes an increase of activity. This is the aim of those who practice mental exercises without spiritual adjustment.

There is a higher plane upon which we may work to the same end. The Spirit of the Christ in us will, with our co-operation, "call" these faculties into activity, as Jesus called His twelve disciples and put them to work in the spiritual realm or kingdom of heaven consciousness.

The love story of Jacob and Rachel is one of the most beautiful in all literature. He served her father seven years for her hand and was then disappointed because he had to marry her elder sister Leah. He then served seven more years, which because of his great love seemed but a few days. Thus the children of Rachel, Joseph and Benjamin, were the last to be born, after love had waited many years to reach a ripe maturity. This would indicate a special significance as attaching to the faculties of imagination, represented by Joseph, and of faith, represented by Benjamin.

The first child born to Leah was Reuben. At his birth she cried, "Jehovah hath looked upon my affliction." The emphasis is on the word "looked," and we find that the meaning of the name Reuben is "one who sees," "vision." Thus the mother revealed the character of the faculty represented by the child, and this is likewise true in the case of each of the sons.

The first faculty brought forth in man's spiritual development is vision or the ability to discern the reality of Spirit that lies back of every form or symbol in the material. Like Jacob all Truth seekers are anxious to develop faith (Benjamin) to remove mountains and imagination (Joseph) to mold substance to their desires, but like Jacob they must first bring forth the faculties of seeing, hearing, feeling, praise, judgment, strength, power, understanding, zeal, and order on the spiritual plane.

Simeon, the second son of Jacob born to Leah,

represents hearing or, in a broader sense, receptivity. When man is receptive to the inflow of Spirit, nothing can keep his good from him and he is in a position to make rapid strides in his development.

When Levi, the third son, was born, Leah exclaimed, "Now this time will my husband be joined unto me." The emphasis is on the word "joined." Levi means "uniting," which in the body is feeling, in the soul sympathy, and in the spirit love. The faculty of feeling or, in a broader sense, love is the unifying principle in consciousness. It connects our forces with that upon which we center our attention. When our attention is focused on Spirit, these faculties become spiritualized. When we elevate love (Levi) to the plane of Spirit (John), it draws to us all that the soul requires. When it is kept on the lower plane as feeling or emotion it often leads to selfishness, to indulgence, even to violence.

The fourth son of Jacob and Leah was Judah. In the Hebrew this name means "praise Jehovah." In Spirit this is prayer, and it accumulates spiritual substance. In sense consciousness this is acquisitiveness, it accumulates material things, and if the self is dominant, it "hath a devil" (Judas).

The fifth son, Dan, was born to Bilhah, Rachel's maid, whose name means "bashfulness; timidity; tenderness." From tenderness comes judgment, the faculty represented by Dan. In its higher aspect this is spiritual judgment and is symbolized by Christ's disciple James, the son of Zebedee.

Bilhah also bore another son to Jacob, who was

named Naphtali. This means "wrestling" and represents strength or stability. The strength center is in the small of the back. That there is a close relation between the physical, mental, and spiritual aspects of strength is shown by the fact that the back becomes tired when thoughts of materiality are held and are greatly strengthened by spiritual thinking. Man retards his spiritual growth by his material thinking and his mental clinging to the things and conditions of the world. All strength originates in Spirit. The higher expression of this faculty is symbolized by Jesus' disciple Andrew.

Jacob and his sons lived many ages before the time of Christ and His disciples, thus portraying the earlier stages of man's spiritual development. They were natural men living by sense and emotion. In the same way our faculties, in the first stages of their unfoldment, express the lower planes of sense. Like everything else with which we have to deal, they have a physical, a mental, and a spiritual side to bring into manifestation.

The faculties evolve on three planes. Jacob being a type of the mental, his sons especially portray the intellectual side of our faculties. By developing along this line we may attain to a high degree of human perfection. But before we can become anything more than human or mortal our faculties must be spiritualized and put to work on the heavenly plane. Just as the sense man has reached his present stage by the development of sense faculties, so the divine man must evolve by the development of spir-

itual faculties. They are of course the same, dif-
fering only as regards the plane on which they are
expressed, since body, soul, and spirit are really one,
and are separated only in consciousness.

Leah's maid, Zilpah, whose name means "dis-
tilling," "extracting an essence," was the mother of
the next two sons, Gad and Asher. Gad symbolizes
power, which at this stage of development is on the
personal plane. Divine Mind gives man power over
his thoughts and ideas and the forces of the soul.
In the higher consciousness this power is exercised
over the self and inner conditions rather than over
other persons and the world without. The higher
expression is shown by the disciple Philip.

Asher symbolizes understanding (Thomas),
which corresponds to wisdom in the realm of Spirit.
The knowing capacity in man acquires a body of
knowledge by study and observation of the world
without. The same capacity acquires wisdom by
being receptive to the Spirit within. Tennyson
brings out this difference clearly when he says,
"Knowledge is earthly, of the mind; but wisdom is
heavenly, of the soul."

Jacob now had eight sons, four by Leah, two by
Bilhah, and two by Zilpah. Two more were born
to Leah and, last of all, two to Rachel. The grouping is suggestive and becomes more so when we turn
to the New Testament and find that Jesus called His
disciples in groups that closely correspond. The
disciples were called in pairs, usually brothers. Jesus
Christ called the brothers James and John the

"Sons of thunder."

There is an interesting story in connection with the birth of the next son. In the Oriental household where there were several wives there were sure to be petty jealousies and naive intrigues. Jacob spent most of his time with Rachel since she was his favorite. To get his attention, Leah bargained with Rachel to keep out of the way for a while and as a reward gave her some mandrakes or "love apples" that her son Reuben had brought in to her. Leah had great zeal and was never discouraged by the failure of her attempts to win Jacob's favor. When the child was born she called him Issachar, which means "there is reward." Metaphysically he represents the faculty of zeal, active in substance and in the body consciousness.

Zeal is a strong force, the urge behind all things and the impulse to every achievement. It sets in motion all the machinery of the universe to attain the object of its desire. It should be tempered with understanding and love, else it becomes a destructive force. Even a criminal may be zealous in his work.

The spiritual side of the zeal faculty is represented by the disciple Simon the Canaanite, who was also called Simon the Zealot. Its center is in the back of the head, the medulla, from which it sends out a strong nerve energy to all parts of the body.

It is worthy of note that Leah, metaphysically the human soul as distinguished from the spiritual soul (Rachel), was the mother of six, or one half of Jacob's sons. The last one she brought forth was

Zebulun, whose name means "habitation," "neighbor," and who symbolizes the faculty of order. Order is the first law of the universe. Indeed there could be no universe unless its various parts were kept in perfect harmony. In the sense mind there is disorder, manifest in confusion of thought and action, while in Divine Mind everything is perfect order. Therefore it is most important, if we are to survive at all, that our thoughts be put in order and kept in harmony with divine perfection.

Even in the small details of life, such as dress, conversation, eating, sleeping, and working, system and order enables one to live a richer and fuller life. But only in divine order can be found the life abundant and eternal. This order is established in our body and affairs when we live up to the highest convictions of our being under the guidance of spiritual understanding. No man-made law can be strong, true, or exact enough to insure perfect order. Only when man becomes conscious of who and what he is can he exercise his God-given dominion and bring his life into line with the principle of divine order, which is mind, idea, manifestation. The disciple James, son of Alphaeus, symbolizes order on the spiritual plane and his throne or center in the body is located at a point just back of the navel.

During all this time Jacob had been serving his father-in-law Laban in the country of Haran. This was a high or mountainous place and metaphysically denotes that high state of consciousness in which the individual is strengthened and given the determination to go forward to spiritual enlightenment and full development. Eleven of Jacob's sons were born in Haran, the last of whom was Joseph, the child of Rachel, the beloved. In the high state of spiritual consciousness man develops the faculties from the simple one of seeing up to that of imagination, the faculty represented by Joseph.

From Haran Jacob went to Canaan, the state of consciousness which to the individual is the kingdom of heaven. From Haran he brought a great wealth of substance, including camels, cattle, sheep, gold, and silver, and even the teraphim (highest thoughts) of that land. Before he entered Canaan, however, it was necessary for him to become reunited with his brother Esau. In other words, the intellect must recognize its relationship to the body and discharge its duty toward this body by supplying its needs. We cannot enter the kingdom of heaven as intellect only or as spirit alone, but must take the body with us, for spirit, mind, and body are unified and one. All must be lifted up.

The last of the sons of Jacob was born after his return to Canaan. Rachel ("ewe" or lamb), mother of Benjamin, represents the lamblike quality of the spiritual soul in its first stage of conscious unfoldment. When this brings forth the active faculty of faith (Benjamin), through its union with the intellect (Jacob), it experiences sorrow and dies; that is, it sinks back into the subconsciousness to await a greater understanding and development. The activity of faith at first seems to a negative soul quality

(Rachel) to be a Benoni ("son of my sorrow").
But this activity means strength and executive power
on the mental side of the individual, and Jacob
changed the child's name to Benjamin, which means
"son of the right hand."

The faculties imagination and faith are more
fully discussed in other chapters.

Mysteries of Genesis

Chapter Eleven

JOSEPH A TYPE OF THE CHRIST

Study: Genesis, chapters 37, 38, 39, 40, and 41.

Affirmative Prayer

I am free from the prison of limitation and lack, and I take my place in the household of the King, where all His resources are at my command.

Joseph a Type of the Christ

MAN, AN IDEA in Divine Mind, is manifested in various states of consciousness. These appear outwardly as personalities and take form as bodies. In describing states of consciousness the Bible uses the personality in a representative sense, with the meaning of the name as a key to the state being explained.

The meaning of the name Joseph is "whom Jehovah will add to." He represents the "increasing" faculty of the mind, that state of consciousness in which we increase in all phases of our character. This is especially true of substance; for Joseph as imagination molds mind substance in the realm of forms. He had a coat of many colors; his dreams were always of forms and shapes—the sheaves of wheat, the stars and moon. An interpreter of dreams, the phenomenal was his field of action. This formative power is characteristic of the imagination, and among the twelve primal faculties of mind we find that this faculty of the imagination is represented by Joseph.

The Joseph faculty is the dreamer of dreams and the seer of visions, which are expressed always in forms and symbols. If you are a vivid dreamer and can correctly interpret your own dreams, you may know that you are developing your Joseph faculty. However, it is one thing to dream and quite another to interpret dreams correctly. All people dream more or less, but few can interpret dreams. Visions come under the same head, for dreams are not necessarily the sole concomitant of sleep.

When a person has developed the Joseph state of consciousness and can give vivid forms to his ideas by using his imagination faculty, he does not take his dreams or visions in a literal sense at all. He rather unclothes the dream of its form by using the same power that he has of clothing ideas with form. Then he clearly sees the idea hidden behind the forms and symbols of his dream. He knows that all forms represent ideas and is able to resolve the form back into the primal idea of Divine Mind. Thus he is taught by Spirit more directly than is the ordinary individual. Spiritual Truth comes to him directly through an always open channel.

One of the surest proofs that a person has opened himself to the inflow of Spirit is that he has symbolical dreams. Divine ideas are being reflected into his mind, and he may mentally see them and catch their import if he meditates patiently and persistently upon the relation that each form bears to ideas. Things are first ideas, then thoughts reduced to the plane of sense perception. If one will still the senses, one can perceive the thought that is back of the thing. This seems a slow way to learn the language of mind, but it is a sure way. When an individual has learned that language so that he accurately translates into thoughts every form and shape on all planes of phenomena, he is indeed a Joseph and stands next to Jesus Christ. Joseph is the great prototype of the Christ, later manifest in Jesus, and a study shows many parallels in their lives.

All ideas require a matrix of substance in which to form themselves and to increase in manifestation. Egypt represents the substance matrix, the body, in man's consciousness. Instead of being allowed to indulge in idle dreams, the imagination (Joseph) is captured by the other faculties (brothers) and sent down into the body consciousness (Egypt), where it is set to work to bring about the eventual preservation and the redemption of the body. This is the work of imagination in the regeneration, and is the allegorical meaning of Joseph's slavery in Egypt.

The other faculties of mind are not always so ready to fall into line and be led by Spirit as is the faculty of the imagination. This is especially true in the earlier stages of our life on the higher or spiritual plane of consciousness. They are the "older brothers" and have been in complete charge of the Father's flocks (thoughts) for so long that they are unwilling to yield their supremacy to this faculty who is but a mere lad and an idle dreamer. The imaginative faculty is often ridiculed. Seeing, hearing, feeling, and the other brothers are "practical" faculties and well able to care for the flocks (thoughts) of their Father (I AM). To sense consciousness imagination seems to be only a "dreamer," interesting to listen to, but only fit for laughter.

In the evolution of the individual as well as the
race, imagination is one of the last faculties to be
developed.   Civilization did not begin until man
began to exercise his imagination.   When he visioned
himself as crossing the sea, the sailboat soon afterward became a reality.   By the exercise of imagination man began to invent, design, plan.   Truth students know the value of visualization.

Joseph was the proud owner of a coat of many
colors, the gift of his father.   The coat is the symbol
of the Truth given us by the Father.   Truth in its
entirety is symbolized by the seamless garment worn
by Jesus, for it cannot be separated into divisions or
parts.   All Truth is one Truth.   Joseph's coat's being of many colors indicates that when we open up
this new realm of consciousness and begin to use the
imagination, our conception of Truth is colored by
the many previous mental states that have so long
herded our flocks of thoughts.   In this stage we
have not yet come into the understanding, the pure
white light of unqualified Truth, which is the seamless robe of unity.

The home of the imagination is in the realm of
ideas, where another dimension of mind is opened
to it, even the kingdom of the heavens.   The imaging faculty gives man the ability to project himself
through time and space and thus rise above those
as well as all other limitations.   Even when the conscious mind is asleep the imagination continues its
activity and we have dreams.

As we have learned we cannot take our dreams

literally but should interpret them by the symbols given us. For instance, Joseph's dream about the sheaves was a dream of substance and a prophecy of his superior consciousness of the universal substance. That consciousness of substance afterward brought forth fruit when he supervised the storage of grain in Egypt, and this grain furnished the needed supply of his father and brothers and brought them to him. Imagination uses ideas to increase its store of universal substance and clothes ideas in form, for it is both an increasing and a formative faculty. Joseph built the bins and stored the corn of Egypt for seven years against a famine.

An uncontrolled imagination will often exaggerate and increase trivial or even unreal things until they distort both body and mind. It is a very powerful faculty, and we must learn to discipline it if we would make it practical in serving our highest good. When Joseph was called upon to interpret the king's dream, he was very humble and said, "It is not in me: God will give Pharaoh an answer of peace." By following the inspiration of the supermind or Jehovah consciousness we can control the imagination and direct its work to practical ends.

Joseph's being brought down into Egypt signifies the imagination's becoming active in the body consciousness and in the subconsciousness. Imagination usually reaches out into the unseen world about us and forms substance on the pattern of our thoughts. But its first duty is to go down into the Egyptian darkness of our material and sense thought and, under the law, lift the body consciousness up to a higher plane. Body, soul, and spirit are unified and one, and the Truth student simply cannot afford to lose sight of this fact that all three are to be lifted up. Unless he is very careful in this regard, the body consciousness may be left far behind the soul and spirit and some unfavorable reaction become manifest in the body or affairs.

Joseph was sold to Potiphar, an executive officer of Pharaoh's court, whose name means "belonging to the sun," "dedicated to Ra." He represents one of the ruling ideas in the state of consciousness represented by Pharaoh, "the sun." Egypt symbolizes the material body consciousness ruled by the sun or by the solar plexus, which is the sun center in the subconsciousness. Pharaoh rules in obscurity or darkness because the great sun of the body, the solar plexus, is obscure or unknown to the conscious mind. The light of the sun of righteousness is veiled by our conscious living on the low plane of sense.

Joseph was tempted by Potiphar's wife and because of her false testimony against him was shut up in prison. The imagination seems always to be getting into trouble for it is so little understood. The sense consciousness of the animal soul (Potiphar's wife) tempts us through the imagination to gratify its sense desires. When its expression is refused there is a reaction and we seem for a time to be imprisoned or limited in making progress. But if we patiently bide our time, knowing that only good can come to us, the seemingly imprisoned faculty

(Joseph) will prove its God-given power.

The fact that Joseph was sold as a slave into Egypt by his brother faculties signifies that man at a certain stage of his unfoldment will barter away his high ideals of Truth in order to go on living in sense consciousness. He will even debase his imagination (Joseph) and send it down into his body consciousness to stir up his emotions and get the thrill of sensation. The faculty of imagination, if it has been trained and disciplined, will however work for the good of man even in the darkened realm of sense that Egypt represents. Though the intent back of Joseph's going down into Egypt was error, yet the result proved to be good. This shows the outworking of the law stated in Romans 8:28: "And we know that to them that love God all things work together for good." Even when error seems to be in the ascendancy, there is that in us which remains true to God and finally brings about our deliverance.

The great point in the story is that Joseph, even when overcome by error from without and sold into Egyptian slavery, still remained true to the high ideas of his father. In any department of life the imagination will work for the development and perfection of the individual or for the direct opposite of this, depending upon how it has been trained. It is a powerful faculty, for it forms ideas in substance and brings desire into manifestation. If the desires are allowed to run riot on the sense plane, the imagination will proceed directly to bring them into outer manifestation as inharmony or disease. On the other hand, when the imagination is kept busy with high ideas, ideas originally inspired in it by the I AM, it is the most effective of all the faculties for the work of spiritual development. Faithfulness to high ideals, when they are coupled with an unshaken confidence in the I AM, cannot be wholly overcome by error, nor can any one who exercises these qualities be kept for long in the background.

By faithfully performing the routine duties intrusted to one, even in a prison, one is certain to be advanced to a better and more remunerative position. But faithfulness has an even greater reward than this, for all the while the faithful one is building a firmer, truer, and more Godlike character in himself, which is an enduring reward, for thus he enters into the possession of true riches, the spiritual consciousness. Joseph was made the overseer of all the prisoners and later was released and given the highest position in the land as prime minister or adviser of Pharaoh.

"His master saw that Jehovah was with him, and that Jehovah made all that he did to prosper." God prospers us when we give the very best that is in us and do all things as unto Him, acknowledging Him in all our affairs. This is a sure way to success, and when success does come we should realize that it resulted from the work of Spirit in us because we made of ourselves channels through which the Christ mind could bring its ideas into manifestation. The true Christian never boasts that he is a self-made man, for he well knows that all that he is and has, together with all that he can ever hope to be or to have, is but God finding expression through him as life.

The name Pharaoh, ruler of Egypt, signifies the sun, or more properly, the reflection or representative of the sun on earth. The Egyptians considered him to be the earthly reflection or focus of the rays from the sun-god Ra; therefore he was "the sun of the earth." The body is a microcosm, symbolized in the Scriptures as Egypt. Therefore we should expect to find somewhere in it a "Pharaoh" or sun center. This is the solar plexus, the sun center of the body, which to the conscious mind is in obscurity or darkness, which metaphysically is Egypt.

Joseph was not only in Egypt, he was also in prison, but we read that "Jehovah [law] was with Joseph." At this stage of development, although our imaginative faculty is already the slave of the lower self, we place still more restriction upon it, keeping it in such complete abeyance that we neither perceive its presence nor obey its promptings. It is completely imprisoned in the depths of the subconsciousness where we have consciously banished it because we thought it a useless and idle "dreamer." But all the while it awaits the opportunity to express itself, for the Lord (law) is with it, and in due time it will come into its rightful place as an important faculty in the consciousness.

The chief butler and the chief baker were also in prison (subconsciousness). This shows how we put the Spirit of life (the butler's wine) and of substance (the baker's bread) in bondage to or under the dominion of the sense man. By this time Joseph had become the warden in charge of all the prisoners, so that life and substance were under his control. When imagination controls these it exercises a powerful influence in the subconsciousness, bringing into manifestation many things that are so foreign and strange to us that they seem to come from without.

The butler and the baker each dreamed a dream, Joseph interpreted both, and in each case it came to pass exactly as he said. This gave him prestige as an interpreter as well as a dreamer of dreams that later brought him to the attention of the king.

What is the significance of dreams? The time of dreaming is either when we are losing consciousness in the process of going to sleep or when we are regaining it during awakening. When we are in deep sleep we live in the subconsciousness, a life of which the conscious mind knows nothing. It catches glimpses of it when we are making the transition from the one state to the other. However, we are in close touch with the superconscious, the mind of Spirit, when we are in this borderland state between sleeping and waking. At such times one who is spiritual-minded and who at all times seeks to know what infinite wisdom has to reveal, receives his message. Spirit speaks in symbols such as the butler's cup of wine and the baker's loaf of bread, and the trained faculty of imagination (Joseph) interprets the symbols to the conscious mind.

When the spiritually awakening man has reached this stage of development there is an increase of energy throughout the body. A great increase of vitality is experienced. As we previously noted, the imagination is the "increasing faculty," since it is constantly giving form to substance. The Hebrew meaning of the name Joseph is "one who increases." The great increase that comes at this stage of development lasts about seven years, or passes through seven stages of activity, symbolized in Pharaoh's dream by the seven fat kine and the seven full ears of corn.

Those who are wise will conserve this energy in the storehouse of subconsciousness, because there is certain to be a reaction proportionate to action. The law holds good for every form of energy. When this generated force is properly conserved, the reaction is not felt. When we exalt the Joseph state of consciousness (as did Pharaoh) and let it rule in our body, the Spirit will show us just how to handle the situation. Then we shall make storage batteries of our "cities," which are the ganglionic centers of the body (Egypt). When Pharaoh gave Joseph the power and authority to do this conserving work, he changed his name to Zaphenath-paneah, a compound word which means "savior of the universe," "sustainer of the life of the world," "governor of the district or the place of stored-up life." This would clearly indicate that the body should be ruled over by the spiritualized imaginative faculty working under the direction and by the power of Spirit.

Mysteries of Genesis

CHAPTER TWELVE

THE I AM AND ITS FACUL-TIES IN THE BODY

Study: Genesis, chapters 42 to 50

Affirmative Prayer

I am Spirit, and I have the power to quicken my spiritual identity in both the formless and the formed substance.

The I AM *and Its Faculties In the Body*

HE BIRTH of Jacob, son of Isaac and Rebekah, is described in the 25th chapter of Genesis, and the remainder of the book, or exactly half of its fifty chapters, tells of the activities of Jacob and his twelve sons. Such emphasis shows the importance of Jacob as a symbol of the I AM, that spiritual man whose creation, manifestation, and development is the theme of Genesis. This ideal man does not fully develop in the Jacob symbol but continues to unfold all through the Bible, coming into full expression as Christ Jesus. As Jacob, however, we find man developing his spiritual faculties (twelve sons) and then taking them down into Egypt (body consciousness) to begin the great work of redemption.

Involution always precedes evolution. The I AM and its spiritual faculties must be sent down into the body consciousness before the evolution of the spiritual man can begin. Spirit does not direct the work of regeneration from a distant heaven, but from its center in the crown of the head directs and transforms the very heart of each atom of the body.

Many Truth students have thought it unnecessary

to go down into this obscure kingdom, the body. Like Peter on the mount of Transfiguration, they would build a tabernacle and remain there. They are not willing even that Joseph (the imagination) should spend part of his time down in Egypt, making ready the storehouses and filling them with the vitality that will be needed when the intellectual man has exhausted his resources. These will find that they cannot have that joyous reunion of mind and body with all its brothers (faculties), unless they are willing to let the higher thought go consciously down into the body (Egypt) to rule there, as Joseph ruled second only to Pharaoh himself.

Volumes might be, indeed have been, written with Joseph as a text. In his history is hidden some of the most interesting of the processes of regeneration. This hidden realm within our organism is an Egyptian or obscured state to most of us. Yet it is a great and important kingdom, whose ruler, Pharaoh, is enthroned at that great nerve center which our physiologists have correctly named the "solar" plexus. They tell us that this is the brain of the body, and that it is the nerve center through which most of its functions are controlled. Psychologists have also given it much study and have discovered that the solar plexus is the organ through which ruling or directing thoughts operate. Bible symbology tells us that it is Pharaoh, he of the "hardened" heart that would not "let the people go."

We must not forget that it is down in Egypt (the body) that we find the "corn" or substance

that is required to sustain the whole man. The
several visits of Joseph's brothers to Egypt for corn
and their final reconciliation with him are a symbolical representation of the manner in which we
make connection with the obscured vitality center
within the organism, finally bringing all our faculties into conjunction with it, that it may in due
course be lifted up to a spiritual manifestation.

Canaan, from which Jacob and his sons mi-
grated, means "lowland," while Egypt means "tribulation." To the metaphysician these names represent the two phases of substance. Canaan represents the invisible substance that surrounds and in-
terpenetrates all bodies, while Egypt represents substance that has been formed as material and is perceived by the senses. The faculties of mind, represented by Jacob's sons, first inhabit the realm of invisible substance and are sustained by it, then they
come into the realm of the visible or formed substance, from Canaan to Egypt. This is the way in
which the mind forms the soul and its vehicle, the
physical body. Thoughts are first manifest as ideas
in the invisible substance, then they enter into visi-
bility as things.

When man is ignorant of the creative power of
his mind, he gravitates to a material basis in all his
thinking or acting. Among the sons of Jacob only
Joseph (imagination) had knowledge of the reality
of the invisible. The others scoffed at him as a
visionary. They refused to plant their seed thoughts
in the soil of the invisible substance and the result

was a famine—there was no corn in Canaan.

When we refuse to observe the creative law of mind, we oppose the working out of life's problems in the divine way, according to Principle, and are compelled to work them out in a harder way. This is why the "way of the transgressor is hard." Thousands go down into Egypt and suffer the trials and limitations of materiality, when, if they were more observant of the law and obedient to their spiritual leadings, they might remain in the joy and freedom of Christ. Yet even in the world of materiality (Egypt) the chosen of the Lord (Israelites) prosper and multiply. The children of Jacob increased from a few score to over two millions during their sojourn in Egypt. No matter how great your trials or how dark your way may seem, if you hold to your belief in the omnipresence, omnipotence, and goodness of God, you will succeed, and no material oppression can hold you down.

Joseph is a sublime idea of Truth that goes down into the darkened sense consciousness, and under the law finally raises it up and out of sense and into Spirit. He was seemingly forced there by his brothers, yet he was sent by the Lord to prepare for the maintenance of Jacob's family through the period of dearth that later came to Canaan. The Truth he represents, when taken down into the sense consciousness, establishes there a new realization of life that will result in the regeneration of the entire man. We must often go consciously into every part of our body and build it up in Truth with new ideas of life and substance.

The brothers of Joseph were greatly troubled when he insisted that they bring Benjamin, their youngest brother, down into Egypt. Benjamin, among the twelve faculties, represents faith. Imagination (Joseph) needs faith to complete its work and to hold fast the gains it has made. We, like the brothers, think that faith is too pure, too lofty and holy to risk its being contaminated with the things of material sense. We like to hold it on the high plane of spiritual consciousness rather than send it down into the body consciousness. Yet this must be done to save the other faculties and the whole man. The brothers were in grave danger of being cast into prison, or so it seemed to them, unless Benjamin should be brought down into Egypt. They remembered their father's great grief over the loss of Joseph, and they felt that the sacrifice of parting with Benjamin, the son of his beloved Rachel, would be too much for him.

During these trying moments their minds recalled Joseph and his cries for mercy, to which they had turned a deaf ear, selling him into slavery. Joseph's immediate presence may have had something to do with suggesting this memory although they did not recognize him. Conscience stricken, they said one to another, "We are verily guilty concerning our brother, in that we saw the distress of his soul, when he besought us, and we would not hear; therefore is this distress come upon us." They evidently understood something of the law of sowing and reaping in those days, for at least they did not lay their troubles to "Providence," as is done so much now. They knew that they were about to reap exactly what they had sown years before.

Reuben, the eldest brother contributed his "I told you so" by reminding the others that he had opposed their evil deed at the time. But Judah was the one who made an effective plea for Benjamin and his father. This is one of the most excellent things of its kind in all literature and is recorded in the 44th chapter of Genesis. It shows a complete change of mind and heart, which is true repentance. It was Judah who had proposed selling Joseph into slavery. The praise faculty, which he represents, had been on a very low plane of expression at that time. But Judah had grown with the years, as the praise faculty grows with use, and had become most unselfish, even to the point of offering himself as hostage for his younger brother. Where selfishness, jealousy, and hardness had before ruled him, there was now unselfish love, humility, devotion to principle, and willingness to serve, even by the giving up of his liberty or his life, if need be, for the sake of his father (I AM).

True repentance is always followed by forgiveness, which is a complete wiping out of the error thought from consciousness and a full deliverance from the inharmony that the error thought has caused. After hearing Judah's plea, Joseph could restrain himself no longer. He made himself known to his brothers, and there was a happy reunion. He sent them home rejoicing, laden with presents for their father, and there was no longer any reluctance about bringing Benjamin down into Egypt. In fact the whole family came unto the place (consciousness) of plenty for all.

True repentance means the changing of the mind and all its contents of error belief. When we have done this we can unify ourselves with Truth, and then we are blessed in both soul and body with the true riches of Spirit.

The seven years of plenty followed by seven years of famine shows that the unregenerate man lives in a consciousness of duality, seeing good and evil, heat and cold, plenty and poverty, feast and famine. The spiritualized imagination, represented by Joseph, sees the whole of life as one. He sees no lack but recognizes a coming consciousness of lack and relates it to the present consciousness of plenty and by this unifying work he lays up a store of substance for future use. The imagination should rank high among all the faculties of man, for without its magic touch life becomes flat, stale, and meaningless; but once imagination is awakened, man is filled with health, life, substance, and plenty.

Joseph was thirty years old when he began his great work in Egypt. At about that age man completes a natural cycle in the evolution of his soul, and is ready for an adventure into the spiritual. Jesus was thirty years old when He began His ministry. Many Truth students have experienced a great spiritual awakening at about this age.

One of the surest proofs that you have opened yourself to Spirit is that you have symbolical dreams. Divine ideas are reflected into your placid soul like shadows on a quiet pool. You see them mentally and you may catch their import if you meditate patiently and persistently upon the relation that each image or symbol bears to thought. Things are thoughts reduced in vibration to sense perception. When you still the senses you will begin to perceive the thoughts that are back of things. This may be a slow way but it is a sure way to learn the language of mind, and in time it enables one to translate all the shapes and forms one sees on any plane of consciousness, into their corresponding thoughts. When this is accomplished one has become a Joseph and stands next to Jesus Christ.

God spoke to Jacob (Gen. 46:1-7) and told him not to fear to go down into Egypt, because He (God) would go with him and bring him out again after that he had become a great nation. Jacob and his sons, together with their wives, children, goods, and flocks descending into the land of Egypt, symbolize to us the unification of the I AM with all the faculties of the mind and the life energy and substance of the whole man. This happy result was brought about by the action of the faculty of imagination, and they all dwelt together in the land of Goshen, which signifies unity.

Thus the father and the brothers of Joseph took up their abode in the land of Egypt and Joseph nourished them there. The imagination, which is our faculty of increase, when established in Truth, prepares the way for us. It inspires, encourages, and sustains the other faculties in us when they come into a seemingly material phase of being, and ultimately brings about the spiritualization of the whole organism, mind, soul, and body.

Joseph brought his father to the ruler, and Jacob blessed Pharaoh. This shows that the power that rules the body, under the material regime, rules in obscurity or is without spiritual understanding. When imagination (Joseph) brings the higher understanding (Jacob) to the body consciousness (Pharaoh), the higher blesses the lower.

Joseph's brothers had been shepherds in Canaan. It is the business of our mind faculties (Jacob's sons) to tend those thought aggregations (flocks, herds) which pertain to our vitality. There were no sheep in Egypt, but Pharaoh made them "rulers" over his cattle. Having come down into a more material state of consciousness, they must take dominion over and lift up the animal thoughts and tendencies in the body. Cattle represent physical strength, which like all the powers of man on the natural plane, must be spiritualized. This is done by a transmutation of quality and is attained by right thinking, or putting the "cattle" under the control of the thoughts of reality or Spirit, represented by the Israelites.

In lower Egypt, during the time of Joseph, was the city of On, perhaps the world's oldest known city. Here was located one of the great temples of

Egypt, whose high priest was Poti-phera. The daughter of the high priest was Asenath, who became Joseph's wife.

Asenath represents the feminine or love side of the natural man. She was the mother of Joseph's two sons. These were Manasseh (understanding) and Ephraim (will), and they inherited Joseph's allotment in the Promised Land (regenerated perfect body). Understanding and will are dominant forces in the race because they are necessary in the development of the soul. If the imagination (Joseph) were wholly free (unmarried or without responsibility), it would indulge in day dreams and fanciful schemes that could not be worked out in a practical world governed by inexorable law. If in this dreamy state the mind is given a definite thought of Truth (such as monotheism, taught at the school of On) and is joined with the natural soul (Asenath), it brings forth the two stabilizing mental qualities will and understanding, symbolized by Joseph's sons Ephraim and Manasseh.

Manasseh means "who makes to forget." He was the first son born to Joseph, who had a great deal to forget. He needed to forget the wrong done him by his brothers, the temptation of Potiphar's wife, and the error of long imprisonment. Thus the son Manasseh stands for denial and represents the ability of our mind to erase and completely forget all error thoughts.

Ephraim means "very fruitful." He represents the ability of man to add to his consciousness what-

ever thoughts he may choose to affirm and to become fruitful in his thoughts even in the land of
affliction. This is the work of will power: Ephraim
wills a thing and it is done.

The very first step for the beginner in Truth is to
set up a new and better state of consciousness based
upon the absolute. He must develop the Manasseh
quality of forgetting the not-good by denial and the
Ephraim quality of increasing the good by affirming
it to be the real. The understanding and the will
must be especially active in one who would overcome and master the sensations of the body, which
is one of the first steps in its regeneration.

When Joseph came to visit his father in the land
of Goshen, he brought his two sons with him.
Hearing that they were coming, "Israel strengthened himself, and sat upon the bed." Thus denial
(Manasseh) and affirmation (Ephraim) bring
strength when weakness is manifest. Jacob blessed
his grandsons, and his blessing is significant. Manasseh, being the first-born (denial precedes affirmation), would be entitled to the chief blessing, but
Jacob laid his right hand upon Ephraim and his
left upon Manasseh, instead of the other way
around. Joseph, thinking his aged father's dim eye-
sight responsible for this seeming error, called his
attention to it. Jacob replied that he knew what he
was doing and that although the older boy should
become great and important, Ephraim (affirmation)
should be the greater of the two. Though denial
is very important in clearing the subconsciousness

of its error, affirmation is more so, for it fills the consciousness with constructive ideas of Truth.

Jacob next called all his twelve sons together and gave them each a separate blessing. Judah's blessing was the most significant: that he should conquer all his enemies; that his brothers should all bow down before him to praise him; and that the scepter of power or ruler's staff should not depart from him "until Shiloh come." Shiloh signifies peace of mind, wholeness, entirety, fullness or completion, and symbolically refers to the coming of the Prince of Peace, the Messiah or Savior. Jesus was a direct descendant of Judah, as is shown in the 1st chapter of Matthew. The name Judah applies to only one of the twelve tribes, but is often used to designate the Jewish nation as a whole. This would indicate that praise (Judah) is such an active principle in spiritual thought that it is deserving of first place. Praise is one of the foundation faculties of man's mind for it relates him directly to the Father. This faculty is quickened and enlarged through prayer and all other forms of religious worship.

In the Scripture allegories the various individuals represent the different phases of character through which one man passes in his spiritual unfoldment. As these follow each other in a series, gradually reaching greater heights, the old phases of character are left behind, replaced by new ones. Thus the Bible characters are said to "die" and to be "gathered unto their fathers." Tennyson was inspired to express a great truth, as poets often are, when he said, "Men may rise on stepping-stones of their dead selves to higher things." So each of the great Bible personalities is gradually replaced in the mind of him who is in the narrow way. When a great change takes place, some old phase of consciousness has lost its hold, and we read that Jacob or Joseph or another character "dies." This does not mean that there has been any loss or that anything has gone away, but that certain states of mind have fulfilled their regenerative work and have been succeeded by others. Joseph also died in Egypt, but not until he had lived in the children of Manasseh and Ephraim unto "the third generation." In other words, the Joseph characteristics gradually become a part of the whole body consciousness.

The Children of Israel are the thoughts of reality or true ideas about Being that have to be brought out in every department of man's consciousness. These true thoughts are for a time submerged (slaves) in the fleshly realm in order that they may bring the body consciousness out of its darkness and ignorance into light and life. It is their mission to lead the whole man back into his spiritual consciousness or Garden of Eden estate. The I AM thought, represented by Jacob (Israel), is at work in the inner consciousness and it will become a great "nation" of true thoughts. Out of this multitude of thoughts will eventually emerge the one, supreme idea-man, perfect and divine, the "only begotten from the Father," the Christ.

Question Helps

for Students of

Mysteries of Genesis

Chapter I

Spiritual Man

1. What is the threefold character and purpose of the Bible?

2. Why do we regard the story of the Creation as an allegory?

3. What is the key to the interpretation of an allegory?

4. How are numbers or figures used in allegories?

5. Explain God as Divine Mind.

6. How does mind create?

7. What is a "day" as the term is used in Genesis 1?

8. What is the "heaven" that was the first creation? What is the "earth" in Divine Mind?

9. What is a faculty? Differentiate among spiritual, soul, and body faculties.

10. Why is light necessarily the first creation?

11. What, in terms of mind, is "darkness"?

12. What is the relation of faith to light, darkness?

13. Is the sun the source of light?

14. What is and whence comes the light of mind?

15. What are the "greater" and the "lesser" lights?

16. What kind of ideas are the "creatures" and "sea-monsters"? How do they differ from "cattle" and "creeping things," and how do all these differ from "birds"?

17. Explain the sequence of creation: light, earth, plants, fish, animals, and finally man.

18. Why was man created last?

19. How does man have dominion over the earth?

20. Explain man as "image." What is the relation of image to idea? to expression? to manifestation?

21. How can an "image" be male and female?

22. How are ideas reproductive "after their kind"?

23. Upon what do ideas depend for sustenance?

24. Why does not man see his own creations as "very good"?

25. Did God create the universe as a thing apart

from Himself? What is God's relation to His creation?

Chapter II

Manifest Man

1. What is your conception of Elohim God?
2. Why is a period of rest necessary to creation?
3. How do we rest spiritually?
4. What is the relationship between Elohim and Jehovah?
5. Explain the difference between "creating" and "forming." What is "reforming" and "transforming"?
6. What was the reason or necessity for the forming of Adam?
7. What elements entered into Adam?
8. What is this "dust" from which Adam is formed?
9. How does the manifest man receive his vitality?
10. Was the giving of life a single, complete act, or is it a continuous process?
11. Explain the metaphysical meaning of the Trinity.
12. Compare the various concepts of the Garden of Eden, and give your own conception of it.
13. What is the metaphysical meaning of "eastward"?
14. What is the "tree of life" in this Garden of Eden which you have explained?
15. What is the "tree of the knowledge of good and evil"?
16. What are some of the other trees?
17. Give the source and course of the river Pishon?
18. What is the work of the river Gihon?
19. What in man relates him to the psychic?
20. Explain how the Euphrates keeps the garden fruitful.
21. How does man "eat" of the trees of the Garden of Eden? How do we "eat" of the word of God? Of Christ's body?

22. Explain how man "fell" by "eating" and how he must regain his perfect estate by eating the "living bread."

23. Why was Eve formed from Adam's rib rather than by the same process that Adam was formed?

24. What was the only time God said "The thing thou doest *is* not good"? Explain the importance of wisdom uniting with love.

Chapter III

The Fall of Man

1. What part does man have in God's creative work?
2. What is the "Adversary"?
3. What results from misuse of the reserve energy?
4. From what and into what did man fall? Was it an event or a gradual process?
5. What does woman symbolize metaphysically and what is her divine purpose?
6. Is it necessary for man to experience "evil" in order to understand life and appreciate the good?
7. We say that evil has no power, yet man is "lost" in a "knowledge" of it. Explain.
8. How does the Christ mind overcome "evil" and lead us back into the kingdom of good?
9. Explain the "fall" of man in terms of cause and effect.
10. What is the "promise" of redemption? Has it been fulfilled?
11. How does error become a subconscious tendency?
12. What is symbolized by the "nakedness" of Adam?
13. What is the "holy marriage" and its fruits?
14. Who or what was responsible for the "fall"?
15. Show how the "curse" upon the serpent (sensation) is being fulfilled by conscience and by man's shame at his actions.
16. What is the metaphysical explanation of the pain of childbirth?

17. What is the "curse" of the ground?

18. Eve represents mother love. Explain.

19. What is the "coat of skins" and what is to become of it?

20. Explain "good" and "evil" as opposite poles of being.

21. What in consciousness is represented by Abel? By Cain?

22. What is symbolized by the offering of sacrifices?

23. What is represented by the death of Abel?

24. What does Cain really fear?

25. Does the Bible teach the eventual salvation of the whole race?

Chapter IV

The Reaction to Sense Living

1. What is the historical value of the Genesis story of the Flood?

2. What is the first indication of a flood in the experience of an individual?

3. Can an individual prevent the manifestation of error thoughts? Can he escape their consequences?

4. What causes cataclysms of nature?

5. What good can be attributed to an earthquake?

6. How do the "sons of God" wed the "daughters of men," and what is the fruit of such union?

7. Explain the law of reaction.

8. What is the reaction of living in sense consciousness?

9. What is signified by 'Lamech and by Noah,' and what is their metaphysical relationship?

10. What are the causes and the results of "crosscurrents" in the body consciousness?

11. What is the origin and meaning of the phrase "ashes to ashes, dust to dust"?

12. How is the balance maintained between positive and negative conditions in the body?

13. What is the cause of "nervous breakdowns"? How prevented?

14. Discuss experimentation versus spiritual revelation.

15. Where and what in the consciousness is the "ark" of the Lord?

16. What is signified by the dimensions of the ark?

17. What are the animals, why "two of every sort," and how are they fed?

18. What spiritual faculty is portrayed by the Flood?

19. How may we assist the I AM in cleansing the true body idea?

20. What do the sons of Noah typify?

21. What is the spiritual "drunkenness" symbolized by Noah's experience?

22. What is meant by Noah's "nakedness"?

23. What is the "curse of Canaan"?

24. Why should one who is consciously regenerating his soul and body give attention to diet, exercise, cleanliness, and the like?

25. Of what is the rainbow a symbol? Explain the rainbow as the bridge between earth and heaven.

Chapter V

The Initial Step toward Redemption

1. What is the "mystery which hath been hid for ages"? From your study of Genesis thus far can you explain "Christ in you"?

2. Why is Abraham taken as representing faith?

3. What is meant by a "plane" of consciousness?

4. Briefly describe three planes of consciousness.

5. What do we mean by "going" to various places or parts of the body?

6. What characterized Abraham before he was

"called," and how does he correspond to the individual of today?

7. How does God "call" the various faculties into activity?

8. Is "blind faith" of any spiritual value?

9. What is the symbology of Egypt?

10. Show how spiritual understanding saves the soul (Sarai).

11. What causes the "plagues" of bodily disorder and death?

12. What is the relation of Abraham and Lot metaphysically?

13. Where in the body of man does faith center?

14. What is symbolized by the return from Egypt?

15. Why must we separate Lot from Abraham in our consciousness?

16. How does the inner meaning of Canaan suggest the immortality of the body?

17. What state of consciousness is "the plain of the Jordan"?

18. What is signified by Lot's captivity?

19. How do we "sow to the flesh" or "sow to the Spirit," and what is the harvest in each case?

20. Why does Melchizedek appear at this particular point in Abraham's experience rather than before or later?

21. Discuss briefly the origin of, reasons for, and results of tithing.

Chapter VI

The Promise of Salvation

1. What turning point does Abraham represent in the story of the race?

2. What became of the souls of those who existed prior to the time of Abraham?

3. How did soul consciousness first dawn in the race

mind?

4. What is symbolized by the nomadic life of Abraham's time?

5. Show the relation between desire and faith.

6. What changes take place in the organism when faith begins to grow?

7. What causes delay in the manifestation of desire?

8. In what way does the desire to develop spiritual powers compare with Abraham's desire to be the father of a nation?

9. What new name is given to the one who overcomes sense consciousness; that is, what name is on your "white stone"?

10. Why does divine revelation often seem vague?

11. What is the truth about "miracles"?

12. Is spiritual healing miraculous? Is it mysterious?

13. When and why was spiritual healing discontinued by the church?

14. How may the church recover its lost power?

15. Trace the steps by which Abraham's understanding of Spirit was developed, and show how God's promises grew more definite in the same proportion.

16. When did God's triune nature become known to Abraham?

17. How did the separation from Lot affect Abraham's growth in faith?

18. What is meant by practicing the presence?

19. What lesson may we get from Abraham as to entertaining "angels"?

20. What is the result of trying to hurry or force the manifestation of God's promises?

21. What is represented by Ishmael?

22. Why does the Abraham of our consciousness plead for Sodom?

23. What is the subtle suggestion of Satan ("the serpent") regarding sensation?

24. How is divine reproduction accomplished?

Chapter VII

The Fruits of Faith

1. Why must the body as well as the soul be saved?

2. Explain: "Christ was the consummation of the aspirations of Abraham."

3. Why was the birth of Isaac so long delayed?

4. What is the meaning of Isaac's name, and what does this show in the Christian life?

5. What effects has the new birth of Spirit upon mind and body?

6. How should "chemicalization" be regarded?

7. How are Isaac and Ishmael opposed to each other, and what must we do with these two phases of mind?

8. What is meant by the banishment of Hagar and her son?

9. Explain how pain caused by the exercise of the natural functions may be changed to joy.

10. What do we really lose and what do we gain when we give up sense pleasures?

11. What in the consciousness is represented by the "land of Moriah," and how may it be productive of good?

12. What is the therapeutic value of joyfulness?

13. What has joyfulness to do with the demonstration of prosperity?

14. What is "the second degree of faith"?

15. What does Rebekah symbolize, and why was she the perfect mate for Isaac?

16. Explain the linking or connecting mission of the Isaac faculty, and compare it with Christ's mediating work.

17. What is symbolized by Abraham's wells, and how are they renewed after a lapse of faith?

18. Who are the Philistines, and where do we meet them in battle?

19. Why are the Philistine thoughts so hard to conquer, and how are they finally overcome?

20. The water of the wells represents the life in the body. Explain how this life stream is generated, struggled for, lost for a time, and regained.

21. What happens to the soul that wins, and what to the soul that loses, possession of Abraham's wells?

Chapter VIII

The Mental Supplants the Physical

1. What phases of life do Jacob and Esau symbolize?
2. What is the significance of their being twins?
3. Is age a just claim to superiority?
4. Is physical strength a just claim to superiority?
5. Why did Isaac love Esau more than he did Jacob?
6. Why did Rebekah love Jacob more than she did Esau?
7. How does soul influence mind to gain its ends?
8. How does intellect gain precedence over the body?
9. What is represented by the mess of "pottage"?
10. What is the "birthright" that Esau lost?
11. What is the importance of the "supplanting" power of the mind in spiritual development?
12. Was Jacob justified in taking Esau's birthright?
13. How does the body react to mind's domination?
14. Why is the inspiration of Spirit necessary to the mind in relation to its treatment of the body?
15. What experience revealed to Jacob that he had wronged Esau?
16. Explain Jacob's fear of Esau.
17. How may we overcome the fear of disease and death?
18. How did Jacob make amends to Esau?
19. How do the faculties of mind ("sons of Jacob") assist in the reunion of intellect and body?

Chapter IX

The Spiritual Gains Precedence of the Mental

1. What is the cause of overdevelopment in some directions and underdevelopment in others?

2. What is "Bethel" in man's consciousness?

3. What is represented by the ladder and the angels of Jacob's dream?

4. What is our first reaction to the thought of omnipresence, and to what changes does it point the way?

5. What should be the true motive for tithing? What is its practical value?

6. Does tithing apply to other things than money? Explain.

7. What does the experience of love contribute to the development of soul, intellect, body and affairs?

8. How does perfect love cast out fear?

9. How does the body sustain itself when the intellect gives it no attention?

10. What is the "inner man" of the subconsciousness with whom the intellect must struggle for control of the body?

11. Why was Jacob's name changed to Israel?

12. What is the real cause of the fear of disease and death?

13. How may fear be cast out?

14. Is the true body subject to material laws?

15. How does the mind project thoughts into the body?

16. Why does the body seem to resist the mind and how may it be trained to accept suggestions?

17. Explain the statement "Yet in my flesh shall I see God."

18. What effect on the body has the recognition of its divine nature?

19. How is the temple to be cleansed and made fit for the I AM?

20. How is "the Son of man . . . lifted up"?

Chapter X

Man Develops Spiritual Faculties

1. What is a symbol? An allegory?

2. How do we find a key to the interpretation of an allegory?

3. Of what is Jacob the symbol?

4. What is the purpose of the allegory of Jacob and his sons?

5. What is a faculty on the physical plane of being? On the intellectual? On the spiritual?

6. What is the significance of the number 12 in the measurement of things, of time, and of stages in development?

7. What is meant by a person's "keynote" or dominant characteristic, and what does it show about him?

8. Should we "specialize" in the development of a certain faculty?

9. What was Jacob's dominant characteristic?

10. What are the stages of evolution in consciousness?

11. Explain the doctrine of nonresistance as it relates to man's development.

12. Explain instinct, intellect, and intuition as they are shown in the three stages of evolution.

13. Why must we study the mind and its action to understand soul and spirit?

14. What is the relation of mind to brain?

15. What are the three methods of developing the mind centers?

16. Which of the faculties are obviously physical?

17. Explain how the faculty of "seeing" operates on the physical, the mental, and the spiritual plane of consciousness.

18. Which faculty is most obviously spiritual? Show that it also has a mental and physical application.

19. Why do we regard praise as an "increasing" faculty?

20. What plane of evolution is especially portrayed by Joseph's sons? What symbols are used to show the development of faculties on the spiritual plane?

21. What is the difference between knowledge and wisdom?

22. What does the grouping of the sons and of the disciples suggest? Which faculties are positive and which negative?

23. To what other faculties is zeal most closely related?

24. What is symbolized by the "death" of Rachel and other characters in the Bible story?

Chapter XI

Joseph a Type of the Christ

1. How does imagination increase our understanding?

2. Explain the part played in manifestation by imagination.

3. Why is Truth revealed in dreams and visions?

4. Dreams are reliable only when correctly interpreted. Explain.

5. What is indicated when one dreams regularly and vividly?

6. How can one get the wisdom or understanding to interpret one's dreams correctly?

7. What is the true body idea symbolized as Egypt?

8. Why is the faculty of imagination so often ridiculed and held in contempt?

9. How is imagination related to the other faculties?

10. In the symbology of Joseph's dreams how should the imagination be regarded by the other faculties?

11. What part has imagination played in the development of modern civilization?

12. Compare Joseph's coat and the robe of Jesus.

13. What is the fourth dimension?

14. What may result from the activity of the imagination when it is not properly controlled?

15. Show how Jacob's special love and favor affected the life of Joseph and, from this, how the I AM controls imagination.

16. Why is it so important to realize and be always conscious of the unity of spirit, soul, and body?

17. What is the true nature and function of the solar plexus?

18. Explain Joseph's imprisonment?

19. How does Joseph's experience and conduct reveal a sure way to success?

20. What subconscious activities are represented by the chief baker and the chief butler?

21. Why does one who is developing spiritually experience a great increase in physical vitality?

22. What dangers are associated with this increase in vitality?

23. How can the life energy be conserved?

24. Explain the seven fat and the seven lean years in terms of the increase and reaction in physical vitality.

Chapter XII

The I AM and Its Faculties in the Body

1. What part of the Book of Genesis comprises the story of Jacob, and what does he symbolize?

2. What is the highest stage of development portrayed by Jacob?

3. What is symbolized by his going down into Egypt?

4. What faculty of the I AM begins the work of regeneration?

5. What faculty is last to go down into Egypt, and why?

6. Why was the solar plexus so named, and how is it symbolized in the Genesis allegory?

7. Explain substance as symbolized by Canaan and Egypt.

8. What causes "famine" in the body consciousness?

9. Why is the way of the transgressor hard?

10. What is meant by the Israelites being the chosen of God?

11. Why did the Israelites prosper in Egyptian slavery?

12. Joseph could not save his people unless Benjamin was brought down into Egypt. Explain.

13. What is true repentance, and what follows it?

14. What causes peaks of prosperity and depression?

15. Does Joseph's experience encourage thrift? Is saving money the same as storing up substance?

16. Why does Spirit speak to us in dreams?

17. What is symbolized by the wives, children, goods, and flocks of the Israelites, and by their descending in a body into Egypt?

18. Why were there sheep rather than cattle in Canaan; and cattle rather than sheep in Egypt?

19. Where was the cradle of monotheism?

20. What faculties are symbolized by Joseph's two sons?

21. What is the importance of denial?

22. Why must denial be followed by affirmation?

23. Why did Jacob give his highest blessings to Judah?

Bible text used in this book, except when otherwise stated, is that of the American Standard Version of the Bible, copyright, 1929, by the International Council of Religious Education, and used by permission.

PRINTED IN U. S. A.

1C-15M-2-36